21st Century Interiors

21st Century Interiors

Edited by Beth Browne

images
Publishing

Published in Australia in 2010 by

The Images Publishing Group Pty Ltd

ABN 89 059 734 431

6 Bastow Place, Mulgrave, Victoria 3170, Australia

Tel: +61 3 9561 5544 Fax: +61 3 9561 4860

books@imagespublishing.com

www.imagespublishing.com

National Library of Australia Cataloguing-in-Publication entry:

Author:	Browne, Beth.
Title:	21st century interiors / Beth Browne.
ISBN:	9781864703658 (hbk.)
Subjects:	Interior architecture.
	Interior decoration—Pictorial works.
	Commercial buildings—Design and construction.
Dewey Number:	729

Edited by Beth Browne

Production by The Graphic Image Studio Pty Ltd, Mulgrave, Australia
www.tgis.com.au

Pre-publishing services by Splitting Image Colour Studio Pty Ltd, Australia

Printed on 157gsm Chinese Matt Art by Paramount Printing Company Limited, Hong Kong

IMAGES has included on its website a page for special notices in relation to this and its
other publications. Please visit www.imagespublishing.com.

Contents

Cultural + Hospitality + Retail

Commercial + Office

There is an increasing focus on materials, flexibility of programming and technology evident in commercial interior design in the 21st century. The range of materials is diverse – exotic wood and new composite materials are employed to great effect and raw materials are exposed to add texture and authenticity. Colour and lighting are key considerations in the design of **Cultural + Hospitality + Retail** spaces: a restaurant might use dark colours and subdued lighting to create an inviting, secluded ambiance, whereas a retail boutique will employ light hues and dramatic feature lighting to ensure the product remains the focus. Theatres, museums and libraries employ acoustics, programming and technology to ensure that information is communicated to visitors in an efficient, accessible and engaging manner.

ABC Cooking Studio

Tokyo and Kyoto, Japan

emmanuelle moureaux architecture + design

ABC Cooking Studios are popular cooking schools located in every major city in Japan and are a popular leisure destination for young women. The eye-catching colours were selected and used for this project not only for the cool, cheerful look, but also to represent a new image for the ABC Cooking Studios.

The cooking tables – custom-designed for ABC – were intentionally located at random in the space to emphasise the casual cooking atmosphere. The tables have a wide variety of colours, enabling students to pick a matching table when they prepare their final dish.

Materials are hard-wearing and easily maintained, including wax-finished vinyl flooring, acrylic enamel paints for the walls and ceiling, and white melamine shelving.

1

2

1&2   Aeon Mall Kyoto Studio
 3   Tokyo Midtown Studio

Photography: Hidehiko Nagaishi

Adour at The St. Regis Washington, D.C.

Washington, D.C., USA

Rockwell Group

Adour at The St. Regis Washington, D.C. provides a dining experience that encompasses a fresh and contemporary interpretation of acclaimed chef Alain Ducasse's cuisine.

Guests can access the restaurant's 25-square-metre foyer directly from the hotel lobby, through The Bar at the St. Regis Washington, D.C., or from the street. Two glass and stainless steel temperature-controlled walk-in wine cases are focal points of the restaurant. The red wine case separates the foyer from the 80-seat main dining room, while the white wine case divides the main dining room from the eight-seat semi-private dining room. The glowing backlit bottles create a beautiful optical illusion – they appear to float within the cases.

The wall opposite the red wine case in the foyer is lined with burgundy-coloured stitched leather cabinetry, as is the ceiling above. Mounted on the wall and ceiling are polished chrome concave discs of different sizes and custom abstract sculptural art installations, designed by the architect and manufactured by Silver Hill Atelier. Custom furniture and art installations from Eaton Fine Art abound.

The main dining room is designed with sensitivity to its historic heritage. Ceiling-height arched windows lining one wall were preserved, letting in an abundance of natural light. The landmark ceiling is composed of carved wooden flowers and decorations, providing an elegant classical contrast to the modern design elements added, such as the Chesterfield-style dining banquettes along one wall upholstered in opalescent white leather and illuminated by rock crystal lamps. Other new additions to the space include three curved wood-wrapped dining niches that contain sleek black, channel-tufted banquettes and metallic wall coverings. Wenge and imbuya wood architectural details are juxtaposed against the matte black lacquer added to the existing woodwork in the space. Off the main dining room is a 20-square-metre semi-private dining room, which boasts a gilded wall covering to complement the polished chrome discs on the ceiling.

1 View of red wine case from main dining room

2 View of main dining room including the three curved wood-wrapped dining niches

1

3

4

3 *Bar at the St. Regis*

4 *Semi-private dining room with handmade gilded wall covering and Burl walnut sideboard*

5 *Dining niche in main dining room with custom art installation in the ceiling*

Photography: Bruce Buck

Andel's Berlin

Berlin, Germany

Jestico + Whiles

This hotel makes a significant contribution to the redevelopment of part of East Berlin, revitalising a former apartment building near Alexanderplatz. This unfinished concrete structure had been abandoned shortly after the wall came down and remained empty ever since. In 2007, following the acquisition of the shell, Jestico + Whiles was appointed as interior designer for this 557-room hotel.

Function and comfort are given equal priority in the design concept. The spaces are uncluttered and crisp but softened by focused textural enhancement. Materials are carefully chosen to be discreet but effective. Colours are fun and stimulating but also calming. Above all, the design is understated but memorable.

Linked to the lobby at ground floor is the grand, double-height, 'Oscar's' bar. Its monolithic stone tile interior is juxtaposed with accents of colour from the lounge furniture and stacked glass bar. The sky bar, in the crown of the tallest corner tower, has 360-degree views of the city. It is a louche and loungy loft space, lined with anthracite polished plaster, scored to reveal a lining of fuchsia suede.

The hotel's 60-seat fine dining restaurant serves gourmet Austrian cuisine. Further dining for more than 500 guests is available in the hotel's two dining rooms, which retain a special, intimate feel through the use of upholstered dividing screens and windows.

The hotel rooms are perfectly considered, crisp, calming and uncluttered. A timeless palette of anthracite, black and white is offset by accents of shocking, saturated citruses. A sheer, raw silk panel mounted in glass connects the bedroom to the bathroom and illuminates as a Rothkoesque artwork when the bathroom is occupied, filtering light while allowing privacy. Stone porcelain tiles in the bathroom are washed by concealed lights to soften the mood further.

1 *Lift lobby*
2 *Main lobby*
3 *'Oscar's' brasserie and lobby bar*

1

2

3

4 'delight' buffet restaurant

5 Executive bedroom

6 'a.lounge' executive lounge

7&8 14th floor 'sky.bar'

Photography: Ales Jungmann

4

5

6

7

8

At Vermilion

New York, New York, USA

Searl Lamaster Howe Architects

A midtown Manhattan restaurant, originally built in the late 1990s was the venue chosen by this Indian–Latin restaurateur. The original restaurant is composed of a 1000-square-metre bi-level space; this cost-effective renovation was developed to use the essential elements of the former restaurant, while reinventing the space for a different menu and a more contemporary venue.

Features of height and openness are emphasised: the bar on the first floor becomes the stage for the dining spaces above. Backlit glass columns, a large light fixture with a metal mesh shade, the decorative metal 'curtain' behind the bar, two-storey stair cables and a water curtain reinforce the verticality of the space.

The upper level provides three dining areas – two open and one private dining room, with glass partitions that separate it from the rest of the dining space. Venetian glass light fixtures were reinvented with new shades in the vaulted area of the second floor. The existing wood floor is refinished in grey stain along with metallic tile accents to create a stark palette that contrasts with the red walls and spicy cuisine. Two pools, one on each level, define the stair at the entrance and the dining areas above.

Acoustical ceilings are concealed by perforated metal to add shimmer to the space. Large photographs of fashion scenes are inserted throughout, reinforcing the owner's vision of a contemporary, feminine rendition of Indian and Latin cultures.

1   First floor lounge – north bar with metal ribbon sculpture

2   Second floor – mezzanine dining room under the new aluminium ceiling

3   First floor entry – reflecting pool and rain curtain at stairs to dining

4   Second floor – private dining room with lit photo and new chandeliers

5   First floor – lounge seating with custom light boxes in background

Photography: Daniel Krieger and Christopher Duff

1

2

3

4

5

Ballard Library and Neighborhood Service Center

Seattle, Washington, USA

Bohlin Cywinski Jackson

This library and service centre are co-located on a gently sloping site adjacent to a new city park, forming a powerful civic face along the pedestrian corridor.

The building's entry is pulled back from the street to make a deep 'front porch' that ties together the library and neighborhood service center under the western edge of the roof. Exterior site furnishings are fabricated from a single sheet of bent steel.

Metal channels above the building's entry mark the spine of the building. A pair of red channels forms a distinct line leading through the lobby, over the reference desk and terminating at a glass-enclosed quiet room. Blue channels parallel to the building face lead to the lobby of the neighbourhood service center. Glass walls provide transparency deep into the public areas of the buildings. The skin bends around the corners, marking the children's area and service centre lobby as special spaces. Cedar-clad boxes containing support spaces are aligned on east–west axes and a periscope integrated into a wall adjacent to the circulation desk offers children views to the green roof.

The glass in the curtain wall has a frit pattern of photovoltaic film that produces shading for the neighbourhood service centre lobby. The windows were designed to be individually metered and low enough that people could closely examine the pattern to emphasise the effectiveness of photovoltaics in the Pacific Northwest.

Anemometers, monitoring wind speed and direction, are integrated on the roof. This information is collected with information about light, energy usage, rainfall and other data and transmitted to LED display panels along the building spines as artwork, making microclimatic conditions created by the building visible. Many other environmental strategies were incorporated, reflecting the library's mission to educate the community in the richness and benefits of integrating green design with extraordinary architecture.

1

1 Green roof shown within fabric of neighbourhood

2 Skylights mark entry points

3 Meters educate patrons on the effects of the sun path and the energy being produced

3

2

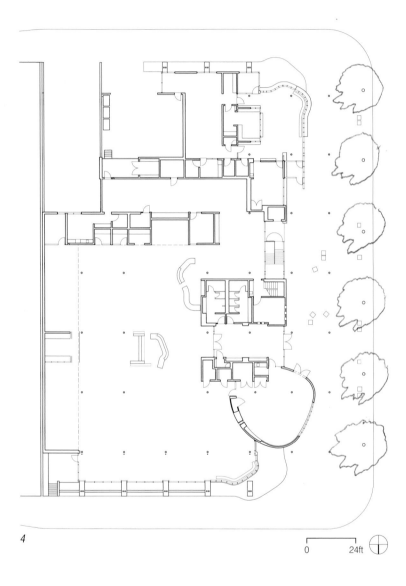

4

4 Ground floor plan; co-location of the library and neighbourhood service
   centre are linked by an exterior porch

5 Reading areas with custom wood furniture designed by the architect

6 Multipurpose room with view to city park

Photography: Benjamin Benschneider (1) and Nic Lehoux (2,3,5,6)

5

6

Banq

Boston, Massachusetts, USA

Office dA

Banq is a new restaurant located in an old Penny Savings Bank building. Divided into two segments, the front area is programmed as a bar, while the larger hall behind serves as the dining area. The design of the space, however, is conceptualised around another division, between the ceiling and the ground.

While the floor needs to remain flexible to accommodate the fluctuating activities of the restaurant, the ceiling contains fixed programs that are part of the building's infrastructure. A striated, wood-slatted system conceals views of the mechanical, plumbing and lighting systems while offering a virtual canopy under which to dine. The geometry of the wood slats conforms to the equipment above, but they are also radiused in order to smooth the relationship between other adjoining equipment, creating a seamless landscape.

Below the ceiling, the functional aspects of a dining space are fabricated with warm woods and relaminated bamboo, amplifying the striped effect already at play throughout the space. Striations of the ground, the furnishings, and the ceiling all create a total effect, embedding the diners into the grain of the restaurant.

Acknowledging the historical setting of the building, the ceiling is suspended from above. Running almost the entire width of the space, each rib of the undulated ceiling is made from unique pieces of 20-millimetre birch plywood adhered together in a puzzle-like scenario. These continuous members are fastened to the main structural ribs running perpendicular to the lattice, tracing both the overall ceiling topography and the steel supports of the base building.

The bathrooms are designed around the fixtures and their equipment: toilets, sinks, toilet paper, among other features, are all ovals. The spaces are covered by monumental oval shells, lit from behind, and are further embellished with other oval features, bringing thematic closure to the space.

1

2

3

1 View from entry

2 View of column

3 View into wine room

4 General view of dining room

4

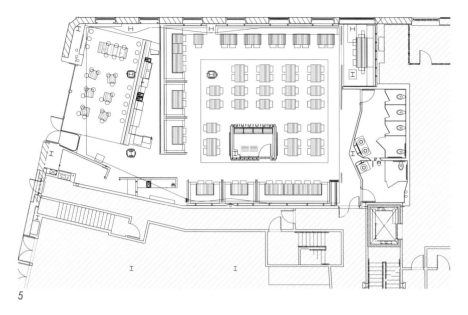

5

6

5   Floor plan

6   Axial view of dining room

7   Lateral view of dining room

Photography: John Horner

7

Benjamin Moore Showrooms

Chicago, Illinois and New York, New York, USA

Searl Lamaster Howe Architects

A design aesthetic was developed for showrooms at the New York Design Center and the Chicago Merchandise Mart, set to open simultaneously. The design was to be flexible enough to be adapted to any future spaces.

Focusing on Benjamin Moore's role as a colour expert rather than a paint manufacturer, the spaces were visualised as a white gallery for displaying its colour palettes.

A new eye-catching, designer-friendly, interactive chip display features square-format colour chips that coordinate with the colours on designers' fan decks. The chips rotate to expose more colours on the back side. The displays are lit by ceramic metal halide track lighting for better adjustability and colour rendering. Different palettes are divided by cabinets which provide storage, and include cut outs for graphics. Graphics can be changed from inside the cabinet, or removed to show product or 3D art.

The white background space provides the necessities for a working designer showroom. The white is articulated with a subtle interplay of circles, squares and stripes. Circle patterns on the floors are reflected on the ceilings with paint colour and suspended acoustical clouds in neutral tones to diffuse sound over the layout space. Designers are encouraged to use the layout tables for putting together palettes. The tables can be pulled apart for smaller groups or moved aside to accommodate larger gatherings.

Both showrooms include a display area for current colour trends, research and inspiration. A technology station is included for designers to utilise colour imaging software. The desktops are constructed of bamboo, for a soft touch, and incorporate a striped texture. Counters have back-painted white glass tops for easy maintenance. White filing cabinets with multiple copies of full colour chips are incorporated into the work areas with chalkboard paint above for signage.

1

1   Chicago showroom – bench opposite reception desk with panels
2   Chicago showroom – mobile work tables with custom lighting

2

3

4

5

3 *New York showroom – work table with chip display beyond*

4 *New York showroom – chip display showing storage dividers*

5 *New York showroom – reception desk and colour technology workstation*

Photography: Matt Wargo (New York); Jennifer Girard (Chicago)

Bijlmer Park Theatre

Amsterdam, The Netherlands

Architectenbureau Paul de Ruiter

This multifunctional cultural building accommodates four users with diverse requirements: a circus (Circus Elleboog), a theatre (Krater Theater), the Youth Theatre School and the Theatre Workplace.

The building is located in the heart of Amsterdam's Bijlmer neighbourhood at the edge of the Bijlmer park, beside the lake. The building is an ellipse shape, with the upper two floors, slightly displaced in relation to the ground floor, providing a covered entrance area. During the day, its striking shape makes it clearly recognisable, while it is conspicuous in the evening because of its colour, which can be altered to fit any occasion with the use of LED lighting. The illumination of the building increases the level of safety and makes the cultural building clearly visible from the urban surroundings.

During the design process, the majority of time was spent identifying the users' requirements in relation to the main auditorium. Circus Elleboog, for example, needed a space with a clear height of 7 metres for acrobatic, trapeze and juggling acts, while the preference of the other partners was for a theatre-style auditorium. A solution was found by designing a rectangular auditorium with two ear-shaped appendages beside the performing area – a circus/theatre auditorium with between 162 and 277 seats. These two rounded areas on the long sides of the main auditorium make it possible to use this space in a range of circus and theatre configurations, by making use of versatile wings and movable seating areas.

In addition to the main auditorium, the cultural building has a spacious foyer, rehearsal rooms, three studios, storage rooms, dressing rooms, a sewing room, meeting facilities and offices.

1

2

1 The theatre seen from the waterfront

2&3 The main auditorium

3

4 Ground floor plan

5 Glass surrounds the main auditorium on the first floor, allowing maximum light when required; the glass can also be darkened to keep out the light when performances are held

6 Main entrance hall

7 Artist René Tosari's carpet design symbolises the diversity of the population of Amsterdam Zuidoost

Photography: Pieter Kers

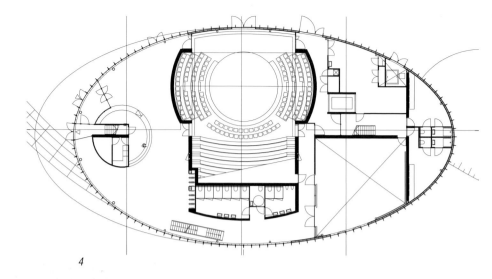

4

5

6

7

bluprint

Chicago, Illinois, USA

VOA Associates Incorporated

Built by master retailer Marshall Field, the Merchandise Mart's history is as monumental as the building itself. Encompassing 390,000 square metres, the Mart extends two city blocks, rises 25 storeys and has its own zip code. An international creative epicentre for more than three million visitors per year, the Mart attracts a clientele with an eye for high design and luxury goods.

In 1945, Joseph P. Kennedy, the father of President John F. Kennedy, helped launch the Mart's status as a mecca for the design industry. Renovations occurred over time, and the need arose for a stylish and sophisticated dining venue, a place where design cognoscenti could meet, mingle and share trade secrets.

Answering this need, the 650-square-metre bluprint restaurant showcases an upbeat, dynamic design that achieves high drama through angular planes, contrasting textures and mixtures of light and dark materials. Performance artist Klaus Nomi and minimalist artist Donald Judd provided design inspiration.

Along the south wall, zebrawood envelops diners sharing an intimate lunch in sculptural booths. The trapezoidal glowing bar is sandwiched by the dark walnut floor and ceiling creating a central sculptural focal point. Along the north wall, mobile panels of blue glass partition the communal dining tables from the bar while filtering colour and natural light. The finished product is a modern space befitting clientele accustomed to high design and sophistication.

1

1 View through the space

2 Bar

3 Perspective view of booths

4 Glass-lined area for communal tables

5 bluprint entrance

Photography: Nick Merrick, Hedrich Blessing Photography

2

3

4

5

Carju Rajah Esthetic Salon, Keio Plaza Hotel

Tokyo, Japan

Elena Galli Giallini

This luxurious esthetic salon is located on the eighth floor of the Keio Plaza Hotel in the skyscraper district of Tokyo. A Middle Eastern, specifically Turkish, design language was used in conjunction with the architectural style of the designer's home country, Italy. Like a traditional Turkish spa, a high, cupola-like ceiling was installed and important symbols from Turkish culture were used as accents throughout the space – the floor of a corridor, for example, features patterns that connote good luck.

The relaxation area, the central space of the salon, connects functionally and visually with a series of autonomous spaces, each with their own function, image and use. The layout promotes a sense of interconnectedness, while at the same time providing privacy and a relaxing environment. The curved ceiling leading down towards the Aqua Zone gives visitors a sense of depth and a warm, cocoon-like feeling of warmth.

The patterns designed specifically for the panels, screens and partitions all incorporate traditional symbols with particular meanings: arches represent life force, tulips represent love, and so on. The rhythmic repetition of these patterns makes customers feel spontaneously connected to the history or tradition invoked in the space, and elicits a natural sense of relief and contentment. The salon was designed with the intention of not only creating a sense of external beauty, but an inner spiritual beauty as well.

Lighting played an important role – at reception, visitors are welcomed by a rhythmic, anticipatory feeling. Other spaces employ natural lighting. In order to create soft shadows, smooth, finished curves were used between ceilings and walls.

1 Reception
2 VIP room
3 Spa – aquazone
4 Relaxation

Photography: Nacasa & Partners Inc.

1

2

3

4

Dolce Vita Porto

Porto, Portugal
Suttle Mindlin

This mixed-use development is adjacent to the FC Porto Dragons' soccer stadium, whose tall concrete walls created an overwhelming presence. Left without scale, generous budget or wiggle room on the site, the architects were challenged to create a breakthrough design that rises above commercial mediocrity.

The concept was an enclosed 'urban plaza', highly visible from the adjacent freeway that provides important connections for the hotel, residential and retail components. The result is a study in transparency, translucency and opacity, with a physical quality to the light that is brought into the spaces through a wide range of glazing systems. The entire structure was designed to provide an environment of changing light and colour, which was an integral part of the architectonics of the building's parti. Suttle Mindlin partnered with T Kondos Associates to achieve the technical solutions for the lighting concepts they envisioned.

The shopping centre is an elliptical, vertical atrium space. Each of the elliptical walkways that project into the atrium space is a bolted, cantilevered, steel and glass structure. Uplights underneath these translucent glass walkways give the translucent glass floors a mystical shimmer; downlights provide adequate illumination for the floor below.

Above this space is a 'folded butterfly' ceiling of perforated metal panels that provides a 'gossamer' effect, allowing some views beyond to the trusses supporting the ceiling. At the lowest level is an elliptical fountain, designed with integral lighting to create a wonderful range of effects including a mist that hovers in the space. Taken all together, these dramatic forms and materials, carefully accented by special lighting systems, create a constantly changing environment.

Awards for this project include the 2009 ULI Top Ten Entertainment & Retail Projects; 2008 AIA Distinguished Building Award; 2007 ICSC International Innovative Design & Development Award; and 2007 ICSC European Design Award.

1

1 The elliptical fountain creates a wonderful range of effects including a mist that hovers in the space

2 The assemblage of glass and lighting systems gives the building a magical quality

3 The spectacular urban complex was designed for destination shopping, dining and entertainment

4 A 'folded butterfly' ceiling of perforated metal panels provides a 'gossamer' effect

Photography: Carlos Chegado

2

3

4

Elixir De Beaute

Melbourne, Victoria, Australia
Holt Clifford Designers

This salon is a space of private and personal indulgence. The interior design aim was to provide a series of visually discrete rooms easily accessed by the therapists. Each room is different so that the spaces are revealed to the clients over multiple visits. While ceiling heights and volumes change, the palette is universal throughout – this consistent finish treatment enhances the spatial depth of the total environment while the ovoid forms create a unique transporting and cocooning effect.

From a planning perspective the space was programmatically challenged. Conventional planning would have led to a cell-like configuration with a perfunctory corridor to access the rooms. By convening a series of ovoid shapes and using the residual space as circulation, the result is a collection of crevices and cool smooth forms, edgeless, welcoming and continually surprising.

The attitude to lighting and fixtures was rigorous and reduced. Each treatment space has a ceiling-mounted fixture that can be focused on the treatment or moved away as mood lighting in a massage setting. The circulation spaces are lit with ball fixtures attached to the curved wall by magnets.

Strong multidirectional beams arc across the curved shapes, detailing and reinforcing the shadowy recesses of the residual space. The only feature fixture is a cluster lamp – a series of raw bulbs of different sizes clustered together – suspended above the desk. Its spare nature adds fragility to the environment and also allows for whimsical seasonal changes to be marked using a change in globe.

1   *Bookings desk with waiting space*
2   *Cluster lamp adds fragility, whimsy and temporal opportunities*
3   *Bathroom contributes to the curvaceous quality of the other spaces*
4   *Walls curve strongly reflecting the myriad spaces beyond*
5   *A large treatment room with tuneable lighting*

Photography: Mark Ashkanasy

1

2

3

4

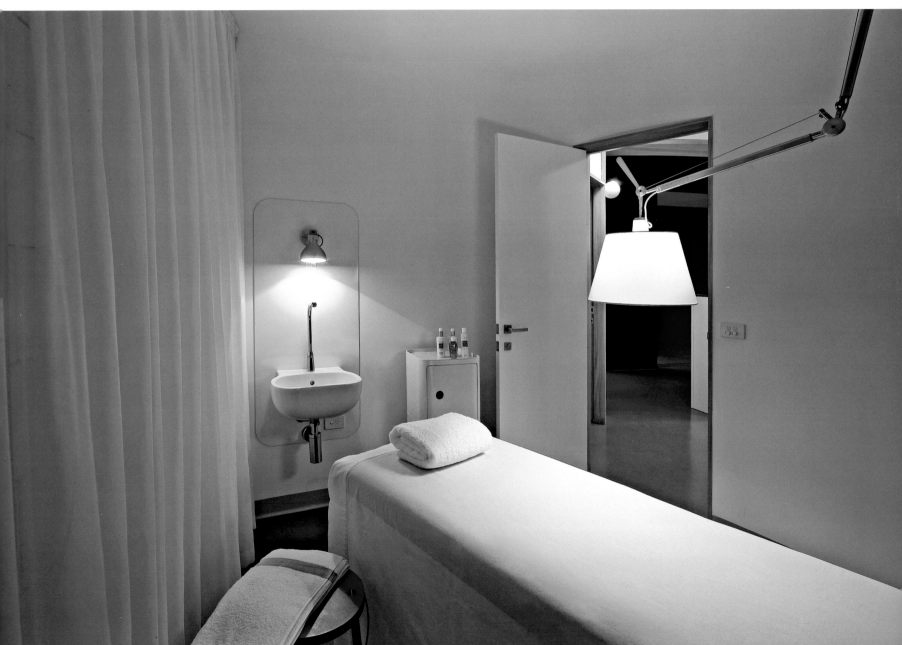

5

Five Sixty by Wolfgang Puck

Dallas, Texas, USA

EDG Interior Architecture + Design

This restaurant at the top of Reunion Tower in Dallas offers an extraordinary take on dining in the sky. The rotating, 150-seat interior embraces a Zen-like sense of stillness and wonder, producing a dining experience in harmony with the spectacular views.

The circular space was brought to life with an ultra-contemporary, illuminated glass bar and stylish lounges. Subtly individualised dining zones play on the drama of the space, making the journey through the restaurant as memorable and interesting as the views.

Guests ascend 170 metres by elevator into the centre of the restaurant. From the entry, the slowly turning cityscape unfolds, viewed between the flamed-granite sushi and robata kitchens on the right and a glass 'ice' bar on the left.

Traditionally, the rotating tower is known for tourists and not for cuisine. To celebrate the view, yet keep guests 'present' to the culinary experience, the design highlights the art of the chef with a central flamed-granite display kitchen where yakitori, sushi and sashimi are crafted 'in the round'. The sculptural host podium balances a slab of polished fir on a block of concrete and behind it a steel-framed screen of stacked river rock allows glimpses of the scene beyond.

A palette of warm grey, ivory and silver lends subtle contrast to the space. Textural, natural materials such as wood, glass, ceramic tile and stone, including locally harvested mesquite floors, provide a grounding landscape for the view. The modern settees, legged booths and armchairs are upholstered in mohair, velvet and leather.

Vertical design elements allow momentary pauses from the cityscape. Panels of glass are embedded with abstracted images of a sand garden; slivers of clear glass connect the eye with the view. Sepia-toned glass screens, embedded with pixel patterns, enclose the energy of the lounge without obstructing the vistas.

1

2

1 Host

2 Lounge and dining

3

4

3   Dining and fire mural
4   Floating bar and lounge
5   Floating bar, sushi and robata kitchen

Photography: Eric Laignel

FUEL at Chesapeake

Oklahoma City, Oklahoma, USA

Elliott + Associates Architects

This restaurant is located on the Chesapeake Energy Corporation campus in Oklahoma City, Oklahoma. Its function is to provide alternative food and a complementary atmosphere to the company's existing Wildcat Restaurant and Conservatory seating area. The architects wanted to convert the existing restaurant into a modern space using high energy and a 'Fiesta' image. It needed to be one of the coolest restaurants in town to satisfy the large number of Chesapeake's younger employees.

The architectural concept was not to create themed spaces, but to create a space that changes with the sun – a space that is liquid with colour, as if you are dining inside a watercolour painting. A stunning range of intense colours complements the food being served: banana yellow, chilli red, watermelon pink and the deep purple of eggplant. The cooking island in the centre of the restaurant is covered in red and green resin panels, like a floating Italian salad. The clean white space is enhanced by T8 fluorescent lamps with colour gels, LED lamps and laminated glass panels with polyester film. Dimmers that control the lighting reduce energy consumption after rush hours.

This new restaurant was designed to enrich the corporate culture of Chesapeake Energy, encouraging employees to remain on campus at lunchtime, boosting productivity and promoting in-house socialisation. The restaurant has become a staff recruitment tool.

1 View of drinks counter, a brick pizza oven enclosed by red Polygal panels and a large plasma monitor that lets diners know when their order is ready

2 East-facing windows and architect-designed tables

3 Dining room with reflection of ceiling light and exterior visible in green glass

4 View east at entry; self-order touch screen on left

5 View south from dining room; self-order touch screen is visible on right

Photography: Scott McDonald – Hedrich Blessing

2

3

4

5

Herman Miller Canada

Toronto, Ontario, Canada

Giannone Petricone Associates

Herman Miller Canada's National Design Centre includes a 900-square-metre showroom organised by a kind of sheath – a 'palette cleanser' made of plywood, a material that is culturally relevant to both Herman Miller and Canada. This tube-like element is defined by a series of butt-jointed fir plywood panels routed in striped patterns to varying depths. This subtractive device exposes multiple grains of ply and brittle adhesive patches in stark contrast with the smooth, pristine bent plywood Eames furniture. This simple technique is surprisingly decorative and provides a degree of dizzying abstraction that transports the visitor from the otherwise mundane outside world.

The showroom is more than a space for display – it includes meeting rooms, lounge spaces and a grand conference area defined by overlapping drapes of heavy wool felt, translucent cotton and flame-resistant sheers. These encircle large light sculptures made from the seats and backs of recycled Eames lounge chairs. The lighting sculptures are meant to evoke sitting under a canopy of beech trees at Marigold, a Herman Miller villa in Zeeland, Michigan where Charles and Ray Eames, Noguchi and others spent much time thinking. The disassembly and then reassembly of these iconic chair parts furthers the representation of plywood, and creates entirely new lighting objects that are automatically imbued with the client's timeless values of innovative clean design, sustainability and quality.

The showroom was the first LEED-certified interior in Canada. Herman Miller Canada was awarded Best of Show in the 2006 Best of Canada Design Competition, a 2006 Ontario WOOD WORKS! Award, a Silver Award in the 2006 DX Awards in the Commercial Interiors category and a 2007 Award of Merit from the Canada Wood Council.

1

1 *Showroom view to coffee station*

2 *Elevator lobby*

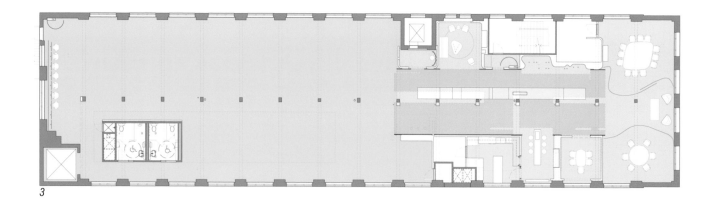

3

4

5

6

7

8

3   Fourth floor plan

4   Showroom view of custom plywood liner

5   Custom chair-back light fixture

6   Showroom plywood liner and custom wallpaper

7   Office floor, view of communal space

8   Sliding door to meeting room

Photography: Richard Johnson, Interior Images

Hotel Romeo

Naples, Italy
Kenzo Tange Associates

The Hotel Romeo was conceived with artistic expression at its heart. Its contemporary design contrasts with the classical style of the city; a calm sense of order counterpoints the raucous swirl of Naples' streets.

Against the classic backdrop of the Gulf of Naples, the entrance to the hotel on Via Cristoforo Colombo leads into the spectacular reception and lobby area. The interior décor includes walls of Macassar ebony hung with works by world-renowned Neapolitan artists Francesco Clemente and Sergio Fermariello. The Music Lounge area includes the discreet and elegant Cigar Room, as well as the exquisite Zero Sushi Bar and Cristallo Bar. Rare items of period furniture are set against more contemporary designs, including those of Antonio Citterio and Philippe Starck.

The hotel's rooms are the epitome of simplicity and elegance – designed in Naples for Naples. Bathrooms are integrated with the room spaces through their semi-transparent screens and complementary materials. The rooms also feature beautiful wood finishes and furniture with exquisite fabrics. The Japanese Suite faithfully reproduces the classic lifestyle of the East with its specially made furniture and outdoor Zen garden. The two bedrooms and living room of the Japanese Suite may be turned into two or three independent rooms if required.

With its backdrop of Vesuvius and the Gulf of Naples, the elements of fire and water provide the theme for the sensuous Daniela Steiner Beauty Spa located on the ninth floor. The tenth floor houses the hotel's gourmet restaurant, Il Comandante, with its bar and a magnificent panoramic terrace commanding great views of Mount Vesuvius and the island of Capri. The room is immaculately presented and adorned with specially commissioned works by artist Lello Esposito.

1 *Entrance*
2 *Daniela Steiner Beauty Spa*
3 *Zero Sushi Bar*
4 *Fireplace*

Photography: Julian Anderson and Richard Bryant

1

2

3

4

Jardin de Jade

Shanghai, China

JWDA/Joseph Wong Design Associates

The Jardin de Jade restaurant was designed and created within the structure of a 1933 historical building in the heart of Shanghai. It is difficult to believe that this 1100-square-metre space was once a slaughterhouse. The structure of the building and its interior layout helped tremendously in the adaptive reuse of the slaughterhouse that was used more than 70 years ago.

The chief architects of this 200-seat restaurant skilfully reused the available space and paid special attention to detail in designing this unique restaurant. The design incorporates images of raw power balanced with elements of understated elegance and serendipitous whimsy. At the entrance, eyes are drawn into the transparent wine cooler and backlit onyx slabs that glow like a fiery furnace. Their glow is also reflected in the dark glossy floors, blurring the boundaries between vertical and horizontal planes.

In the lounge, life-size sculptures of horses separate the seating areas, symbolising the traditional value of impeccable service. Historically popular artwork is also incorporated into the ceiling and wall panels to evoke Shanghai in the 1930s. Natural elements such as stone, metal, fabric, glass and light are deftly woven together to create a mesmerising ambience. The Jardin de Jade Restaurant honours history and tradition, but also revels in contemporary freedoms and design possibilities. It offers a unique and restful environment for customers to experience culture, appreciate design and enjoy the fusion of history and contemporary dining.

1 View of entrance
2 View of the entrance with backlit onyx slab
3 Entrance to dining room with high ceiling
4 Entrance view leading to the dining area

1

2

3

4

5

6

7

5 View of dining space

6 View of corner dining space

7 View of lounge dining space

8 Historically popular artwork is displayed on the ceiling panels

Photography: Kerun Ip

8

Kiribiri Lounge Café

Mestre, Venice, Italy

Filippo Caprioglio
Caprioglio Associati
Studio di Architettura

This 80-square-metre project was supported by a general renovation plan, the objective of which was to restore and reconstruct a previous urban fabric in the historic city of Mestre. The main building of the complex is late-15th-century Gothic. The façade is characterised by three barrel vaults, with ogival arches on the ground floor, an order of windows with rounded arches, with a central trifora, a tripartite Venetian Gothic arch window on the second floor, and a final order of windows with a slightly vaulted architrave on the third floor, corresponding with the attic.

The project's commercial space hosts a new lounge café, Kiribiri, that is conceived in a contemporary style but with a great deal of respect for the existing structure. The principal materials, glass and steel, are used sparingly.

The focus of the project is the lightened counter and the glowing tempered glass box that hosts the toilet facilities. The furniture, custom made for this lounge café, is made from brushed stainless steel and glass, as are the two principal glass lamps.

The two central columns organise the space, dividing the bar counter and the glass box on one side and the couches and tables for clients on the other.

The atmosphere is soft and cosy due to the balance between the new materials and the old structure of the palazzo.

1

1 Main view of the glowing glass counter

2 Side view of the counter

3 Internal view with reflection of the original structure

4 Internal organisation of the lounge bar

Photography: Paolo Monello

2

3

4

Lane Crawford Beijing

Xicheng District, Beijing, China

Yabu Pushelberg

This department store at the Seasons Place Shopping Centre in Beijing is unconventional in every manner. With strong features designed to intrigue guests and passersby, the three-level space seamlessly fuses fashion with architecture and contemporary art with sculpture, tantalising the senses.

Encompassing 73,000 square metres, the store is a study in sculpture and contrasts: black and white, silver and glass, organic and manmade, rectilinear and curved. Each department is uniquely designed with exotic materials, finishes and handcrafted techniques composing a visual language.

At its hub is an atrium where full-colour spectrum fibre optics and streaming video are projected, bringing interactive technology to the forefront of the design. Similarly, a moving belt draws attention to the back of the store, constantly transporting shoes, t-shirts, small toys and other objects to grab the attention of the youthful and trendy clientele. Art was an integral part of the architect's design vision for this glittering space, which is filled with three-dimensional pieces by contemporary artists.

While each section of the store presents a tone appropriate to the merchandise, the overall simplicity and high colour contrast is a constant throughout, allowing the products to 'pop' and remain the focus. Serene and open with marble surrounding walls, the cosmetics section creates a spa-like sense of peace. In the men's clothing department, charcoal walls with sections of charred wood are set against lit backgrounds, with a refined subtle sophistication. Soft curves and free forms with silver linings evoke a sensual 'floating' feel for the women's clothing department.

1 *Store façade*

2 *Custom jewellery display*

3 *Colour glass globe room for home accessories*

4 *Stairs*

1

2

3

4

5 Luxury goods display

6 Men's shoe department

7 Women's apparel

8 Women's accessories

9 Men's apparel

10 Jewellery cases and back wall

Photography: Evan Dion

5

6

7

8

9

10

Mauboussin US Flagship Store

New York, New York, USA

Rockwell Group

In renovating this five-storey townhouse into a high-end jewellery store, the architect created an experiential environment in which guests can discover imaginative fashion jewellery. With the objective of evoking an emotional connection between the customer and the jewellery, the architect focused on playfully displaying the merchandise and capturing the magic of the brand with many layers of surreal and unexpected design details.

Even before entering the store, visitors find a glass vitrine with a trompe l'oeil effect framing beautifully lit jewellery cases. Inside is a dramatic corridor with a sparkling glass wall on one side and another glass vitrine on the other. After opening hours, an interior kaleidoscopic projection – custom-designed to illustrate the magic of the colour and geometry of the jewellery – is visible to passersby.

The journey through the store commences on the first floor; a dark dreamscape space provides a dramatic backdrop to the spotlit coloured lifestyle jewellery glittering in glass treasure boxes. At the entry, a bouquet of stars features the company's signature rings.

The architect played on the traditional notion of a townhouse with walls clad in dark sandpaper with copper stitched mouldings. For a twist on this classical reference, the stitched mouldings are not complete, adding to the surreal nature of the environment. In the centre of the space is a sparkling, faceted glass wall rising through all three retail floors.

The sales pods are intimate areas identified by comfortable wingback chairs and custom-designed ceiling features such as sparkling beads or rich tulle to provide privacy for the store's patrons. To proceed to the upper floors, one can either take the grand stair, or the elevator, which surprises the shopper when the doors open as it is designed as a little personal boudoir or powder room complete with a dressing table, pouf and mirror.

1

2

3

4

1   *Second floor salon*

2   *Lifestyle jewellery displayed in glass*
    treasure boxes against a sparkling cracked
    glass feature wall on the first floor

3   *Bridal floor sales area with tulle ceiling*
    and feather screen

4   *Treasure box displays centred on a*
    backdrop of lace framed panels

Photography: Barbel Miebach

Mint Museum of Toys

Singapore

SCDA Architects

Singapore's toy museum is located along Seah Street, facing the side entrance to the historic Raffles Hotel. The site, a former shophouse, is just 5.5 metres wide and 27.5 metres long. Planning regulations limited the height of the new building to five storeys.

Flanked by two shophouses, the front and the rear elevations of the new infill building are designed to control the amount of natural light entering the exhibition spaces. The mint-condition toy exhibits are sensitive to UV light, with prolonged exposure causing the exhibits to deteriorate and their colours to fade.

The solution to the problem was to design the façade of the museum with glass exposed on the edge. A series of 26 curved-edge glass panels placed on edge and sandwiched between aluminium panels extends from the second storey to the roof of the building. This allows a controlled amount of light into the exhibition spaces through the edge of the glass. The curved-edge glass provides a crystalline façade that is simple yet dynamic as one passes in front of the building. It is symbolic of a clean modern box that houses the antique mint condition toys within.

Entry into the museum is through a ramp overlooking a high-ceilinged café below. The double volume provides for large exhibits and connects the basement café to the street level. A column-free space is created internally and a series of double- and triple-volume spaces are interlinked with a lift and stair core. In section, alternate floors vary spatially, permitting smaller spaces to be 'toy boxes' with controlled interiors that are juxtaposed within large-scale volumes of light-filled space overlooking the street. The rooftop, which will be used for events and functions, is designed as an open terrace with views over the urban landscape.

1

1   Front façade at dusk

2&3   Highlighted exhibits

4   Illuminated display units showcasing exhibits

2

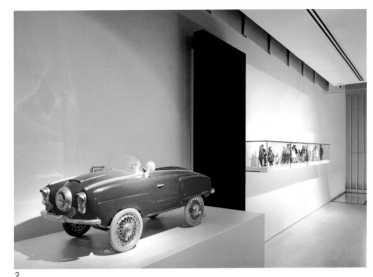

3

4

5

6

7

8

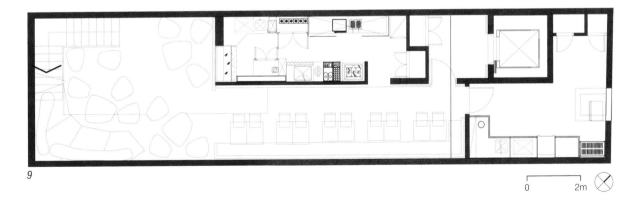

9

0   2m

5 Highlighted exhibits

6 Stairway connecting the galleries on the different levels

7 View into basement café from entry level

8 Detail of custom-made furniture at reception area

9 Basement floor plan

Photography: Aaron Pocock

Nobu Dubai

Palm Jumeirah, Dubai, United Arab Emirates
Rockwell Group

This design is an evolution of many of the concepts developed for the flagship Nobu 57 restaurant, including an emphasis on craftsmanship, natural materials and storytelling. Large-scale computer-generated woven panels surround the restaurant walls and ceiling, creating a fluid, curvilinear environment for dining within the Atlantis The Palm Hotel.

A 20-metre-long curved river-rock wall and a laser-cut metal screen of cherry blossoms mark the entry to the bar. The bar is made from 10-centimetre-thick solid timber planks with a backlit onyx front. For the lounge, the architect developed curved translucent flower panels with cast images of custom large-scale cherry blossom photographs by Michael Palladino, which form an elliptical shape around the centre of the space to create an area for private events.

Three-dimensional woven abaca panels surround the main dining room, creating an experience akin to being immersed under an ocean wave. Guests sit on uplit woven banquettes formed by these colourful panels cascading down from the ceiling towards the floor.

Juxtaposed with the curving fluidity of the abaca panels and their translucent forms is the rectilinear sushi bar. All surfaces of the sushi bar are encased in black bamboo-embedded terrazzo. A white bamboo proscenium forms a theatrical backdrop for the sushi chefs at work. This space is flanked on one side by a blue frosted mirror service bar, and on the other by a curved plaster wall encrusted with metalwork flowers encasing the private dining room.

Wooden arches greet the guests entering the private dining room. The walls of this space are covered with glowing sake bottles and custom artwork on two sides. Overhead, the metallic ceiling is punctuated with a glowing composition of custom suspended pendants.

1   *Semi-private dining alcove in main dining room*
2   *View across main dining room from entry to dining room*

1

3 View of bar with backlit onyx die wall

4 One of two private dining rooms

5 View of sushi bar facing main dining room

Photography: Eric Laignel

4

5

Pacific Ink Tattoo Studio

Terrigal, New South Wales, Australia
Zaia Architects

Tattoo studios have long been regarded as unclean, unsafe and confrontational to the general public. The architects' challenge was to 'repackage' this type of space and redefine both public perception and the spatial impact for the end user. This unique project sets a new standard for a public space where design has rarely been considered important.

The overall design philosophy stems from the key requirements of functionality and product image/public perception. The vision was to create a highly contemporary space that is classy, inviting, safe, clean and fun. Spatial quality, interesting materials, colours, security systems and user interaction modules combine to meet these aims.

Functionally, the approach is very simple with the overall interior area divided into three zones: public, tattoo application and utility. The main public and tattoo areas are designed in an open plan arrangement for interaction, with integrated furniture and materials defining the spaces. Tattoo spaces can be sectioned off from public areas with a retractable screen for more private applications.

References to tattoo history and metaphor are threaded into overall themes to engage the user and pay respect to an industry steeped in cultural significance.

Warm bluegum flooring and wall cladding in the public zone is contrasted by a slicker contemporary palette of stainless steel, whites and charcoals to the tattoo area. High-gloss piano-black polyurethane frames modulate the interior, conceal the structure and visually unify the public and private spaces.

Ceiling panels in corrugated zinc pay homage to a more robust resolve required by the recipient of any tattoo, while contrasting with cleaner, glossier materials. Mirrors are implemented for function and visually expand a relatively small space.

Sound, security, lighting, computer and power systems were configured into the overall design, ensuring user function and visual interest is of the highest calibre.

1

2

3

4

1 *Touch screen and display module*

2 *Historical modules*

3 *Public zone*

4 *Tattoo application zone*

5 *Inspiration images and mirror*

Photography: David Benson Photography

5

Primehouse Restaurant

New York, New York, USA

Yabu Pushelberg

The design intent for Primehouse New York was to reinvent the traditional steakhouse – evolving a classic venue into one with a modern, less masculine ambiance. The décor is quite striking and instantly evokes memories of classic Manhattan – the black and white tiles, the antique mirror tiles, the vintage serving and furniture pieces and the 1950s refurbished pendant light fixtures.

Spatial planning and flow were just as important to the designers as the actual materials that were incorporated into the space. Each of the restaurant's rooms has its own distinctive feel, and as guests move through the space, the rooms transform from dark to light and back to dark again. Further reinforcing the movement of the space are the many patterns that are used throughout – the rooms are not reliant on colour but on patterns and materials that help to create the mood. Most notably is the high-contrast floor pattern of black slate and limestone that has been water-jet cut into a unique circular pattern.

1

2

3

4

5

1   Lacquered host stand

2   Main dining room with vintage ceiling pendants

3   Booths in main dining room

4   Main dining room

5   Custom-designed dining chairs by Munrod in restaurant bar

Photography: Evan Dion

PVR Mulund

Mumbai, India

Jestico + Whiles

This six-screen multiplex cinema is located at the Nirmala Lifestyle Shopping Centre, in the inner suburbs of west Mumbai.

The six screens are laid out symmetrically with three on either side, leaving a cavernous space below the cinema boxes for the ancillary spaces of the multiplex. A frameless toughened glass wall with two sets of glass entrance doors forms the 'façade' of the multiplex, giving shoppers a grand view of the colour-lit sculptural spaces inside. The central spine, consisting of the entrance foyer, concessions counter and the food court, seems to be carved out from below the rakes of the auditoria seating, resulting in a dramatic three-storey-high cathedral-like space.

A ship-shaped conical structure at the multiplex entry features four entranceways carved from the curved and acutely inclined walls. This central structure, painted entirely in white and coloured only with red and magenta lighting, hovers over an island concessions counter. The ceiling of the central space is formed with a three-tiered curved blade arrangement, painted white, following the incline left by the cinema seating. Concealed red cold cathode lighting in the ceiling coves washes the entire installation with a red glow.

Immediately to the left and the right of the main entrance, two red elliptical spaces with comfortable and cosy built-in seating provide meeting and greeting space. These atmospheric spaces are identified with elliptical stone flooring and red cold cathode lighting.

The curvature of these elliptical spaces instigates a curving wall that flanks the foyer on both sides, dipping and turning with a surface that seems to define space without boundaries. Secondary elliptical spaces painted in deep purple 'break out' of the curving surface to announce each cinema entrance. The lavish use of 'Omani' and 'Dark Emprador' Italian marble, rich red 'Stargaze' reconstituted stone, stainless steel panelling and trims, and wenge veneer lends a distinctly five-star feel.

1

2

1 Main lobby

2 Entrance foyer

3 Ticket counter

3

4   Floor plan

5   'Candy Bar' counter

6   Lounge seating

7   Auditorium entrance

8   Main lobby

Photography: Ales Jungmann

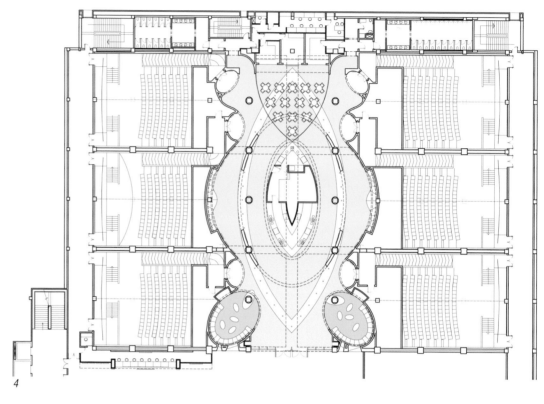

4

5

6

7

8

RED Prime Steak

Oklahoma City, Oklahoma, USA
Elliott + Associates Architects

Ensconced in Oklahoma City's elegant 1911 Buick Building, RED Prime Steak is a world-class vision of modern restaurant design. The architectural design takes full advantage of 5.5-metre ceilings, skylights and sheer volume to create spectacular urban beauty and drama. Each table offers an exciting vantage point for memorable dining experiences. The spectacular wine wall, some 55 bottles tall by 130 bottles wide, separates the bar from the main dining room with shimmering light. These create energy and light that refract off the building's rustic walls.

The rays of light frame a dramatic procession for patrons entering the main dining room. The focal point is the exhibition kitchen where a red portal highlights the activity and a glowing grill. Exiting the main dining room reminds guests of another of the company's signatures, the spectacular wine wall.

The project offers private dining venues – each is a one-of-a-kind setting. Suspended above the historic Buick Building's original automobile turntable is a sleek, red-lacquer, super-private retreat for memorable events, which seats nine. In the Red Room, visitors slip behind the translucent red fabric panels that separate this private venue from the main dining room. It is secluded, yet the view adds an exciting dimension to the dining experience. The 2.5-metre private round booths are in high demand and referred to as 'Tall Tables'.

1   Main entry, west elevation
2   View of bar from entry

3

4

3 Procession detail looking south

4 North dining area with toilet form and Mez on left

5 Procession looking west towards bar

Photography: Scott McDonald – Hedrich Blessing

Scandinave Les Bains Vieux-Montréal

Montréal, Québec, Canada
Saucier + Perrotte Architectes

This urban spa provides a thermal therapy experience that engages each of the body's senses. The design distills the idea of cool glacial forms and the warmness of volcanic rocks and articulates the duality through both the spaces' forms and the selection of various materials.

In this unique environment, walls, floors and ceiling are slightly angled according to a notion of interior topography. Just as in a natural landscape, slight undulations in the ground plane create gentle slopes; depressions in the floor level generate basins of water for bathing; volumes emerge from the ground to sculpt zones for the sauna and steam bath.

Uniting the main space is an undulating wood ceiling that echoes the movements of the floor: walls of white marble mosaic appear to melt at the point of contact with the warm-coloured wood on the ceiling, resulting in accentuated architectural reveals. Heated, cantilevered benches made of black slate offer visitors a warm place to pause in between hot and cold bathing cycles.

Opalescent glass admits natural light through the building's existing openings while providing a sense of privacy. Along de la Commune Street, a thin cascading layer of water flows on glass surfaces, filtering views so that from the exterior, passersby can see only shadowed silhouettes of the figures within the hot bath.

Technically, the most critical area of the project was the bath area where significant moisture is generated by the hydro-jet and steam baths. For these spaces, white Italian marble mosaic was used on the walls and floor for its water-resistant properties. The complex ceiling geometry was developed using 3D-modelling software; the space gained between the existing concrete slab and the new, undulating wood ceiling was a practical solution for the installation of the ductwork and other mechanical systems.

1

2

1   Steam bath

2   Suspended cold rinsing shower

3   Relaxation room and juice bar

4   Hot hydro-jet bath and cold rinsing tub with waterfall

3

4

1 Hydro-jet bath
2 Cold tub
3 Cold shower
4 Steam bath
5 Sauna
6 Juice bar
7 Relaxation room
8 Dressing room
9 Reception
10 Office space
11 Massage room
12 Staff room

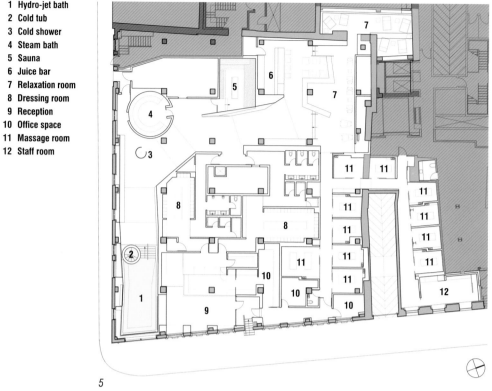

5

5 Floor plan

6 Reception desk

7 Sauna

Photography: Marc Cramer

Sculpture Therapy Centre

Levent, Istanbul, Turkey

Habif Mimarlik

The spaces in the Sculpture Therapy Centre are arranged in accordance with the requirements of the treatment rooms and their sizes. The primary materials used are natural stone, timber (for flooring, ceilings and doors) and transparent glass.

For each area, different practical criteria were taken into consideration, especially regarding choice of materials and also in terms of atmosphere. The ground floor, which functions as the spa floor, was designed in a completely different way from the other floors in relation to materials, colours, the music system and lighting features. Massive timber doors, ceilings and wood blocks enhance its atmosphere. The Pilates room, which has been designed as a different section and made out of glass, is also located on this floor.

The upper floors are home to the treatment rooms and are clean, simple and white. A prototype design, which includes a mirror, hooks, a washbasin and a cupboard, was created for these rooms to provide for the needs of customers and staff. The same prototype was adapted for each of the rooms according to their size.

A more feminine scheme was applied to spaces such as the make-up room and the waiting room, which feature pink wallpaper, sculptural white railings and 'flying' fabrics.

Lighting design makes a dramatic impact on the space. In most of the therapy rooms, hidden lighting details have been applied to create a spiritual atmosphere. Wooden panels in the ceilings of the entrance and spa floors are used for the lighting design and to create a natural ambience.

1

1   *Entrance/reception*

2   *Spa floor, main hall*

3   *Ayurveda treatment room*

4   *Entrance waiting area*

Photography: Gürkan Akay

2

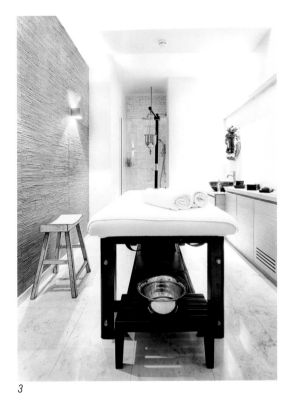

3

4

Segundo Muelle Restaurant

Mexico City, Mexico

Ezequiel Farca

Segundo Muelle, Spanish for 'Pier 2', is a Peruvian restaurant chain with locations in Mexico, Panama and the US. The architect was asked to design the very first restaurant to establish the look and feel of the interior. The design concept, flowing from award-winning chef Daniel Manrique's seafood-rich menu, expresses the architect's interpretation of an upscale, modern coastal aesthetic.

At the entry, the visitor steps on rough floors of board-formed concrete, emulating the patina of a well-worn pier. A dramatic water-mirror adds a hint of ocean ambiance, and alludes to the restaurant's cuisine. Taking cues from traditional Peruvian piers made of concrete, wood and steel, the architect crafted thick machiche wood tables over steel bases, lined the walls with wood panelling and designed concrete tile floors in four different shades of grey.

Divider walls constructed out of roughly stacked timbers play with the light, absorb sound and exude warmth. Complementing the rich palette of structural materials, the architect designed seating with light-coloured fabrics and machiche bases. To complete the experience, he selected flatware, dishes, linens and crystal to harmonise with the surroundings. Special glasses were chosen for the traditional Peruvian tequila, Pisco.

The design utilises modular panel systems on the walls and ceilings so that the design can be easily replicated and scaled for the company's other planned locations. Furnishings in the restaurant's Mexico City location intentionally target the traditional three-hour Mexican business lunch client; comfortable, oversized armchairs invite guests to eat and linger.

1   Entry hall

2   View from entry

3   Table detail adjacent to the bar

4   Stacked-timber wall detail

5   Dining room

Photography: Paul Czitrom

1

2

3

4

5

Smyth Tribeca

New York, New York, USA

Yabu Pushelberg

The most recent addition to the edgy Thompson Hotels collection, Smyth Tribeca on lower West Broadway, provides an urban refuge for the hip in Tribeca.

For this property – Yabu Pushelberg designed the hotel lobby – the firm selected modern interiors with a classic twist, drawing inspiration from the vibrant surrounding neighbourhood. The space resonates with a romantic notion of an elegance of years gone by and the ambience reflects a fine balance of wit and refinement.

The materiality speaks to that of a fine, tailored bespoke suit – pairing sumptuous pin-striped fabrics with a curated collection of custom and vintage furniture and collectibles, such as the colourful clock and robot collections. A sense of craftsmanship can be seen in each and every vignette, creating an eclectic sculpted lobby for all guests to enjoy.

1   View of entranceway and elevator bank
2   Vintage toy robot collection behind reception desk
3   View of hotel lobby bar

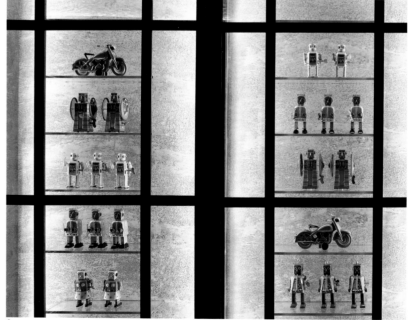

3

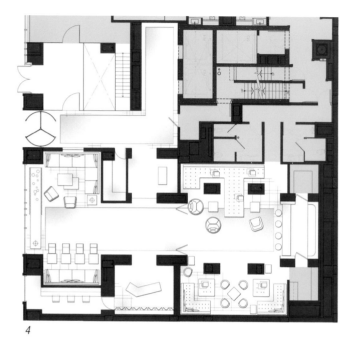

4

4 Floor plan

5 Intimate seating area in lobby/bar

6 Front window of lobby, looking out onto West Broadway

Photography: Evan Dion

5

6

The Source by Wolfgang Puck

Washington, D.C., USA

EDG Interior Architecture + Design

The Source by Wolfgang Puck is the signature restaurant at the Newseum, an interactive museum dedicated to news. The restaurant interior, like the building it occupies, plays with the notion of transparency as a metaphor for freedom of speech and freedom of the press. The three-level space provides three distinct experiences within a unified design expression.

The design thrills in its exploration of transparency – from the dynamic stair and glass balustrade, frosted-glass catwalk and two-storey, temperature-controlled glass wine wall that unify the main floors – to the transparent light fixtures, which reveal their working mechanisms and light bulbs. The look is continuous and contemporary. A palette of white, ivory, taupe and brown suggests peeling away layers, taking the visitor deeper into the story. Wood-framed wire cloth screens create the illusion of privacy while bouncing warm light around the rooms.

On the lounge level, white terrazzo tile floors contrast with chocolate-brown furnishings. Smokey, acrylic pendant lights are clustered over the communal table, with individual pendants along the window wall. Legged booths and settees have a casual, modern feel, inviting impromptu gatherings. Rosewood details provide a warm counterbalance to the minimal interior.

Upstairs, the palette is reversed, with dark wood floors, taupe-coloured leather dining seats and plush, cut-pile settees. Translucent screens section off intimate and more open seating areas. The open floor plan creates service challenges, which the design meets by weaving service into the experience. Glass and stainless steel shelves display the restaurant's glassware and decanters, visually reinforcing the extensive wine program. Individual service stations (for POS systems, flatware and napkins) are designed like pieces of furniture. A large group of acrylic pendants hangs at the top of the stair, floating mysterious light to both floors.

1

1 Bar
2 Stair
3 Dining detail

Photography: Eric Laignel

2

3

Tiffany's Wall Street

New York, New York, USA
Yabu Pushelberg

When Tiffany & Company hired Yabu Pushelberg to transform its newly acquired Wall Street store – located in the Trust Company of America bank building, originally built in 1907 – into a luminous, contemporary retail space, the firm opted for sleek glass-and-metal fixtures and accessories that highlight the sparkling merchandise without compromising the historic interiors.

Boasting 10-metre ceilings and towering marble walls, the 1000-square-metre space entices modern consumers with several key design features, including the winding central staircase (made of glass and Vermont stone), its connecting L-shaped mezzanine and the 18-metre-long mesh and crystal light sculpture created by German designer Ingo Maurer.

In order to divide the grand space on a more intimate scale, a series of stainless steel-clad frames and glass partitions were introduced, creating several free-standing rooms that not only meet the rigorous criteria of the New York State Historic Preservation Office, but also facilitate the privacy needed for a big-ticket purchase. Strategically placed LED and halogen lights reflect off the room's many crystal pendants to create a glittery jewel-box effect unlike any other.

1

2

3

4

5

6

1 Hanging crystal light sculpture

2 Millwork and display

3 Architectural and display lighting

4 Glass chip walls concept developed in collaboration with D'Art

5 Swarovski crystal hanging installations

6 Stair

7

8

7 Glass and metal screen

8 Leather wall finish

9 Ground floor plan

10 Mezzanine floor plan

11 Overhead view of store from the mezzanine level

Photography: Evan Dion

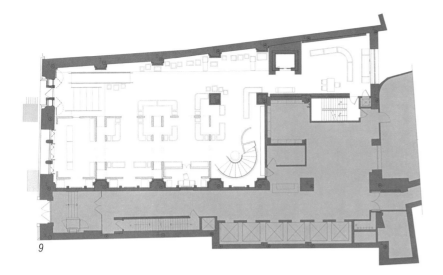

9

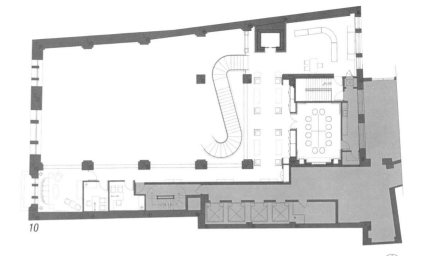

10

11

WakuWaku Hamburg

Hamburg, Germany

Ippolito Fleitz Group

This new restaurant chain's philosophy is grounded in the consistent implementation of the concepts of sustainability and good-value, healthy food that is prepared extremely quickly. The architect's task was to translate the principle of sustainability into an overriding architectural concept.

The space is divided into two main zones: the dining area and the service area. The latter comprises an order counter, kitchen and a take-away area as one unit, which acts as a room within a room. It is painted a strong shade of violet – the restaurant chain's corporate colour. Two digital menu boards suspended from the ceiling display the current menu and images of the food on offer. The colourful, lacquered surfaces form a dynamic contrast to the expanses of stainless steel and the service counter, with its natural white mosaic tile surround.

The dining area makes a sweeping statement with a floor-to-ceiling bench that runs the entire length of the room. The bench wall forms a strong parenthesis and draws patrons into the depths of the space. It is also a content carrier: a gallery designed by Stuttgart-based artist Monica Trenkler unfurls across its entire length.

The severity of the long bench is broken up by chairs of many different origins, forms and colours – their sheer variety creates a friendly impression and their individuality enlivens the room. All the chairs' legs have been dipped 20 centimetres into the corporate colour, which serves as a connective element.

Under the glass roof a row of plants grows out of the rear wall, forming a living part of the furnishings. An innovative lighting system dynamically adapts the lighting tone depending on the amount of daylight. As a result, the restaurant is always perfectly lit and appears inviting from the outside and atmospheric inside.

1   A strong shade of violet is WakuWaku's corporate colour
2   The structural edifice of the service area acts as a room within a room

1

3 This part of the restaurant area was once a courtyard and is now contained beneath a glass roof

4 An alcove containing a table for four is inset in the wall

5 Two- and three-dimensional collages and pictures pick up on the typical WakuWaku leitmotifs

6 The chairs are of many different origins, forms and colours

Photography: Zooey Braun

3

4

5

6

Yew restaurant + bar

Vancouver, British Columbia, Canada

EDG Interior Architecture + Design

An overnight success, Yew – named for the rare, indigenous Pacific yew tree – is a revitalised social centre for the Four Seasons Hotel and downtown Vancouver. Its Pacific modern architecture joins the urban and natural landscapes of Vancouver with contemporary lines, lustrous wood and rough-hewn stone. Yew offers different experiences and focal points within a single, soaring venue, achieving breakthrough success without the cachet of a star chef. In addition to dining spaces, the restaurant now encompasses a generous, 21st-century bar that is standing-room-only many nights of the week.

The winning design utilises locally crafted materials, furnishings and artwork – as well as imagery inspired by nature – to highlight the property's Pacific Northwest identity and give Yew a distinct personality. EDG worked with local artist Brent Comber on the natural wood slab tables and sculpture.

Freestanding design elements, such as the floor-to-ceiling sandstone firebox, the glass-walled private room, heavy timber booth enclosures and the double-height back bar create intimacy while screening views from the hotel. Wood panelling, wood slats and medium-density fibreboard panels carved with treescapes warm the space while tempering existing glazing.

The designer placed a glass-walled private dining room directly under the pyramid skylight. Wood louvres and a tumbling glass sculpture focus and enhance the skylight's effects. This private room has become the 'power table' of Vancouver, generating more money for the hotel than if the designers had filled the entire area with tables. Wine wall storage adds privacy and reinforces Yew's extensive wine offering, much of it from the Pacific Northwest.

Yew has quickly become one of Vancouver's top restaurants as well as a thriving downtown destination. Within the Four Seasons chain, the project serves as a new model for the creation of an exciting, profitable, in-house restaurant without outsourcing to a star chef.

1

2

1 Entry and host

2 Bar, lounge and display kitchen

3

3 Bar and lounge

4 Communal dining

5 Dining, glass-walled private room

Photography: Eric Laignel

4

YMCA Renaissance Center

Detroit, Michigan, USA

McIntosh Poris Associates

For this state-of-the-art fitness centre the architects organised the space so that private areas, such as offices and locker rooms, were kept to the interior of the space, allowing cardio machine users to take advantage of the incredible view of the river while working out.

Recognising the wide variety of group exercise classes offered, the architects created one interior group exercise room to cater for more vigorous activities, while the other room was reserved for more serene practices, such as yoga. Glass walls framed with wenge-stained oak enclose the exercise rooms and offices, maintaining an open, airy atmosphere. Maple sport flooring in the exercise rooms adds a light and gleaming contrast to the dark-stained custom glazing, which provides an ordered datum through which the chaos of moving bodies and machines can be seen.

The main challenge of the space was how to negotiate the pattern of columns, raw concrete and the tangle of HVAC pipes and ducts that were necessary to serve the towers and Wintergarden. The architects turned to art to solve the problems of the difficult space and to create a singular gesture that defines the project. Starting from the lobby, a vibrant mural wraps around the folded planes of the central wall that encloses the locker rooms. Painted by Barney Judge Studio, the colourful mural depicts abstracted nature scenes. The contemporary pastoral scenes, combined with the architectonic faceted planes, give a calming and energetic feeling to the space.

Entrances to the locker rooms are accented with sophisticated grey porcelain tile. Glass mosaic tile contrasts with the stone for a serene combination of green in the men's space and amber in the women's.

1 Entrance introduces the colourful mural
2 Work-out areas feature outside river views
3 The mural travels through the space, and is visible from exercise rooms
4 Dark-framed glazing acts as an organising theme
5 Maple sport flooring cushions exercisers

Photography: Michael Collyer

1

2

3

4

5

Creating an attractive and inspiring workplace is a practical investment in productivity and an effective means of retaining valued employees. Considered programming and planning provides flexible and appealing areas for private and group work and facilitates the development and sharing of ideas. In successful **Commercial + Office** spaces general and feature lighting, acoustics and colour all have a positive effect on mood and concentration, while materials, furniture and finishes can be used to make a statement about a company's philosophy or history. A unique office interior is an essential part of a company's branding strategy, making a positive impression on clients and providing an edge over competitors.

Adobe San Francisco

San Francisco, California, USA

Bohlin Cywinski Jackson

This new headquarters complex for 700 employees spans an entire city block and comprises a historic structure, a parking garage and a new office building that includes expansion space to house more than 900 employees. The first phase of the project was the renovation of the historic Baker & Hamilton building.

The 20,000-square-metre, three-storey, heavy timber and brick Baker & Hamilton warehouse building is a registered San Francisco and California Historic Landmark. During the renovation, the large floorplates were subdivided into thirds with massive brick-bearing walls and structured by a dense grid of large old-growth heavy timber columns and beams. The plan is organised around an original lightwell at the centre of the building. On the first floor, this lightwell terminates at the ceiling into a pyramidal skylight that brings daylight into the building. This central zone at the first floor is known as the 'Town Hall' and includes an arrival lobby and security registration area, a café and large espresso bar and the company post office. Flanking the Town Hall are training rooms, a focus group research facility, a 35-seat digital screening room, a 90-seat auditorium, large video conferencing meeting rooms and a film and sound recording studio.

On the upper floors, new vertical circulation is cut into the existing floors to facilitate movement between software labs, server rooms and software engineering teams. Open teaming areas located in corners of the building become the 'backyards' of neighbourhoods of workstations. The integration of technology throughout the historic building creates a state-of-the-art, yet human-scaled, workplace for employees. This building, along with the approach Adobe takes in operating this facility has earned it a LEED-EB Platinum rating from the US Green Building Council.

1   The historic brick and Colusa sandstone façade is restored

2   Building arrival lobby includes a custom-designed reception desk made from timbers salvaged from the building's structure

3   First-floor 'Town Hall' space for social functions under the historic skylight

Photography: Nic Lehoux

1

2

Agnico-Eagle Mines Offices

Toronto, Ontario, Canada

Taylor Smyth Architects

When Agnico-Eagle Mines Ltd., an international growth company with a focus on gold, approached Taylor Smith Architects to design a new head office, it was occupying the top floor of a five-storey building with dramatic views of St. James Park and cathedral. Working with the architect, the company decided to stay in the building and expand it to 1600 square metres, rather than relocate.

In order to minimise disruption, the project was designed to be built in two phases: first to build out the fourth floor to allow the company to relocate, and then to gut and reconfigure the fifth floor, complete with a new interconnecting stair. The design makes subtle references to the client's core business. At the reception area, the back wall is composed of smooth slabs of horizontally grained travertine that abstractly evoke the geological strata of a mine. Embedded in the wall are random gold-coloured bars. A glass display case contained within the wall showcases chunks of raw mining material. This wall rises up two floors where the slab was cut open to accommodate an open stair that leads to the main boardroom.

Opposite the reception area, the view is terminated by a feature wall composed of stone cores from the boreholes made during the mining process. Mounted vertically, this multi-coloured stone creates a unique, richly textured composition. The rest of the material palette was chosen to provide an elegant, dignified impression. Bamboo flooring was selected for key areas due to its environmentally friendly features. The elevator walls and floor are clad with light-coloured limestone and cherry is used on doors and frames.

1   Reception area
2   Café/acrylic screen
3   Stone core wall
4   Travertine display wall

Photography: Ben Rahn/A-Frame Inc.

1

2

3

4

AMP Offices

Melbourne, Victoria, Australia

Gray Puksand

This workspace for a wealth management company aimed to achieve a sense of connection, to engender communication and to foster a community within the workplace. Management was aware of the need to communicate and to be nimble; staff were committed to reduce stratification, though without sacrificing privacy.

The design provided a series of nooks that act as pinch/decision points linked by a subtle change in floor finish and lighting. This effectively ensures people travel along the designed routes and hence avoid the traps of encroaching upon individual privacy. All routes lead to the light-filled 'town square' or European-style marketplace that becomes the centre of the community. The town square has elements that reflect the urban style and laneways of Melbourne and also includes a 'bocce' pitch and an arbour. All these elements link the space to the outside, taking the focus away from the enclosed glass box that is the modern office building.

Sight lines were considered to provide glimpses of the spaces as the user travels through the large 3800-square-metre floor plate. Nooks deal with the short-field focus, while the atrium provides the long-field focus.

Materials and detailing were integrated to the sustainable resources used. A language was established to link all the zones, and critical to this language was the use of Eco-Core flooring and ceiling product that uses FSC-certified timber. Polycarbonate cladding and timber mullions replaced traditional glazing to the quiet rooms to treat them as markers within the space and move away from expected solutions within a workspace. All fabrics selected were of renewable resource components, all boards were EO or FSC certified. All paint finishes were zero-VOC and all flooring selected had sustainable properties. All selected furniture was GECA (Good Environmental Choice Australia)-certified or had high sustainable properties.

1

2

3 Town square
4 Staff zone connecting to public face
5 Transition between neighbourhoods

Photography: Peter Clarke, Latitude

4

5

APRA_AMCOS Office

Sydney, New South Wales, Australia

Smart Design Studio

The new offices for the Australasian Performing Rights Association + The Australasian Mechanical Copyright Owners Association (APRA_AMCOS) are located in a five-storey timber-framed brick warehouse in inner Sydney. Each floor plate accommodates several departments within APRA_AMCOS, with 95 percent of staff accommodated in open-plan workstations. Glazed offices and meeting rooms are located against the building's cores, with casual breakout spaces in a sunken floor area adjacent to the void and dotted across the floors.

A raised access floor throughout the building allows for concealed and flexible reticulation of services, in turn reducing the visual clutter of the space and allowing the timber beams and joists to be exposed in their original form. To further highlight the building's features and to minimise energy usage for lighting, the use of colour has been restricted to white joinery and workstations, with charcoal wall panelling. Throughout the office floors however, a bold orange carpet was selected to ensure the space remained both serviceable and lively – the warm reflected light gained from the floor surface counters the cool effect of fluorescent lighting.

A new high-level atrium roof contributes to the building's natural ventilation capabilities, and a rooftop terrace forms a private area for small functions and staff recreation in association with the boardroom and function spaces on this floor. The existing trusses have been exposed and painted white to introduce a lofty 'boat-house' feel, a departure from the typical corporate approach to the function of these spaces and a means of distinguishing between the office levels below that are visible through the void. In contrast, the ground-floor conference spaces utilise a darker palette with untreated black steel wall cladding and splashes of colour to generate a raw and edgy space that naturally feels akin to the organisation's association with the music industry.

1

1 *A grand stair takes the visitor from the entry to reception at the heart of the building*

2 *Flexible media room adjacent to the café*

2

4

5

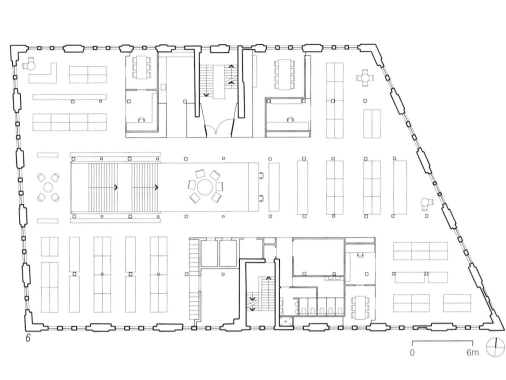

3 The dramatic four-storey void provides visual connection between floors

4 Visitors arrive at a relaxed reception area on level one, at the heart of the building

5 An open-plan work environment is organised around transparent offices and meeting rooms

6 Level 1 floor plan

7 An in-house café at street level provides an opportunity to get away from the desk environment

Photography: Sharrin Rees

6

0   6m

7

Architectural Design Studio

Sydney, New South Wales, Australia

fitzpatrick+partners

A heritage space was stripped, restored and reconfigured to create this single-space design studio, which immediately expresses the vibrant atmosphere created by staff–client interactions and activities upon entry.

The heart of the space is the central zone, which stretches from the entry to the client presentation space. It is defined by a single blue Tretford rug over the original oak flooring and a series of translucent fabric ceiling panels hung below the restored mini orb and pressed-metal ceilings. This space contains the reception zone, informal meeting and reference libraries, as well as the zone for a future stair to link to another level. This ensures that the space is constantly being used, further enhancing the sense of energy and activity.

The client presentation room has a suspended perforated metal ceiling, which is backlit for general lighting as well as visually terminating the central zone. The ceiling also houses lighting tracks, motion and level sensors and projection facilities to allow for all formats of presentation. Timber furniture has been used within this central zone to create an intimate and relaxed setting.

Nestled between the fixed low-level linear joinery storage units are the project-team spaces and single director workspaces. The project teams are situated at Vitra Joyn workstations accommodating groups of six to eight people – the average team size. The defining joinery units are also used for storage of files, project samples and reference materials, and the top surface is used for drawings and models.

A disconnection between new fittings and the fixtures of the original building is intentional. Wiring is looped below arched openings, and ductwork and light fittings are suspended below the original ceilings. New glass walls are located below the original steel roof beams.

1   Central zone of studio
2   Client meeting room
3   Reception desk in central zone of studio

Photography: Eric Sierins

1

2

3

ASIC (Australian Securities & Investments Commission)

Melbourne, Victoria, Australia

Gray Puksand

To suit its business plan, the client suggested a 'cheeky' workspace, one that would provide employees with a desirable environment and a space that is flexible and adaptive to facilitate large movements of staff at immediate notice.

The architects provided an open-plan solution, where the ASIC Commissioner would sit in the same workstation set-up as the latest graduate. Conscious of the floor plate, where the distance between the lift core and the perimeter is relatively small, they established a radiating work plan that circulates around the central core containing the utilities and support meeting rooms. The space between corners creates a tension between the built form and negative space. These smaller areas form intimate workspace zones that support team environments.

To increase the tension between built form and space, the central solid form is carved up by freeform openings. The curved form is enhanced by the adoption of strong colours, strengthening spatial arrangements.

As five floors have the same layout, and given an employee may relocate to different floors several times a year, the architects used a different colour scheme on each floor (red, yellow, orange, blue and green). The juxtaposition of strong bold finishes such as a feature pebble-crete wall against the more sleek and refined detailing of high-quality automotive paint finishes and the feature technology screen within the foyer are a play on the concept of 'strength versus corporate sleekness'.

The detailing and selection of materials were based on ESD principles to help maintain an improved environmental quality to the workspace and minimise health risks during construction. Low-VOC materials, paints, carpets, E0 or E1 board meet government standards. An upgrade and implementation of energy-saving principles was adopted throughout, including the inclusion of energy-efficient lighting, motion-detection switching, improvement of controls to mechanical services and water-saving appliances.

1

2

3

1   'Guitar' utilities

2&4   'Bus Stop' breakout

3   'Hockey Stick' community hub

Photography: Peter Clarke, Latitude

4

Barclays Global Investors

San Francisco, California, USA
STUDIOS Architecture

Barclays Global Investors' wanted its new headquarters to embrace innovation within a professional environment through thoughtful, sophisticated design. This space also needed to provide the infrastructure necessary to meet the firm's significant technological demands.

Connectivity – between the building and the urban streetscape outside, and within the building itself – was key to this project. Vertically stacked blue glass meeting rooms and red-walled collaboration zones are clustered along the southwest corner of the building, engaging and activating the busy entry plaza, and creating a beacon of colour and energy. An internal open glass-tile stair runs the height of the building, reinforcing connectivity between floors; slot windows offer 'peek' views into the staircase and out into the work areas from within.

Responding to Barclays' desire for interaction and openness, the design intersperses break areas within work areas and offers a variety of meeting spaces, from casual to formal. Low workstation partitions, glass-fronted offices and dozens of glass conference rooms convey a sense of transparency; dark-blue glass meeting rooms allow for privacy while still offering views of the action within.

Located at the heart of the headquarters, the trading floors are linked by a three-storey, glass-encased stair that appears as a light box between the floors, providing vertical connectivity and energising the space.

The top-floor executive conference centre takes advantage of the building's unique architecture by creating all-glass volumes set within the double-height space. The minimalist palette of pale limestone and white plaster walls communicates both elegance and serenity. Clusters of pendulum lights appear as small constellations set against sweeping views of San Francisco's financial district.

1

2

3

1   Entrance lobby with lounge and conference room

2   Collaboration zones include conference, coffee areas
    and casual meeting space

3   Ramp at lobby hovers over blue LED lighting

4   Tenth-floor executive conference centre

4

5

6

7

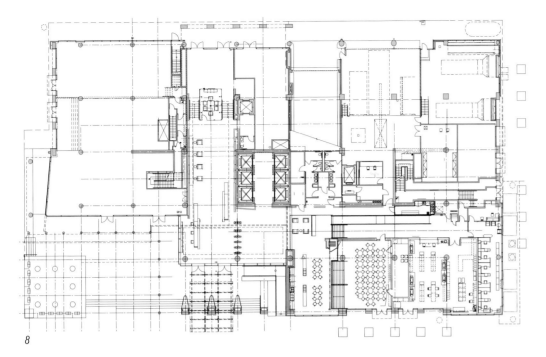

5 Double-height break area overlooks eighth-floor roof garden

6 Central all-glass stair connects trading floors

7 Constellation of lights over executive conference centre

8 Ground floor plan

9 Open office environment with curved metal ceilings

Photography: © Benny Chan/Fotoworks

Baroda Ventures

Beverly Hills, California, USA

Rios Clementi Hale Studios

This 380-square-metre, two-storey brick office building originally included ground-level retail space and a maze of small offices above. Extensive reorganisation resulted in a large executive office with private restroom, a conference room, a reception area, nine private offices and four open workstations. Kitchenettes and restrooms are offered on each floor. Courtyards on either side of the building provide informal gathering spaces for employees and visitors, while an exterior staircase connects the two levels.

The architects adopted a combination of retro and contemporary styles for the renovation of the two-storey Baroda Ventures office. They applied several themes throughout the design – classic modern furnishings with unexpected fabrics, elaborate ceiling medallions and doors with escutcheons, glossy surfaces and repeated patterning at various scales – while incorporating plentiful daylighting. Timeless elegance was achieved by pairing traditional essentials with the latest in design to create a place of sophisticated opulence.

A custom-designed steel-and-glass staircase provides access to the second floor, affording uninterrupted views of the fountain below. At the top of the staircase, through a wooden door adorned with an exaggerated escutcheon, is the reception area, featuring a two-seat Eames sofa in striped upholstery and an aqua leather Barcelona chair. The ceiling was removed and restructured to expose the existing hip roof. New skylights were installed to bring views of the sky and daylight deeper into the office. Interior walls are clad with either white back-painted glass, limed oak panels or modern versions of tongue-and-groove, which function as textural foils for the existing masonry shell.

1   An exaggerated door medallion welcomes visitors

2   Glass-fronted offices maintain an open feeling

3   Executive's office is both retro and modern

4   Conference room features various decorative brass motifs

5   Reception area is skylit from original hip roof

Photography: Tom Bonner

1

2

3

4

5

Bayside Project Management Office

Melbourne, Victoria, Australia

Robert Mills Architect Pty Ltd

The client is a sophisticated residential developer in the business of creating homes and promoting particular lifestyles. Its philosophy is grounded in excellence, with quality construction and sound investment value. The brief was to embody these principles in a physical form.

The design needed to reflect the dichotomy of home and industry and showcase the client's values. With this in mind, the architect forged a link between the sophisticated commercial interior space and a warm residential environment representative of the client's product.

The idea behind this project was to bring together two restrictive areas and create one that had a sense of open space while retaining some intimacy.

Philosophically, the design is all about balance. Chiaroscuro effects create interest and the interplay of light and dark with hard and soft surfaces allows a petite workspace to expand and contract.

The design uses a sophisticated mixture of warm materials and textures. The palette of dark timber, white walls and feature lighting creates a dramatic atmosphere, transforming the space into a boutique-style office, symbolic of the client's work.

The visual flow is continuous throughout the office with the clever use of low-level shelving and a sliding partition wall. The space is confined, minimising the use of heating and cooling. Track lighting allows the user to apply lighting to different workable areas thoughout the office, conserving energy.

1   Workspace

2   Meeting space

3   Floor plan

4   Open-plan office converts into two separate areas utilising a sliding wall partition

Photography: Shannon McGrath

1

2

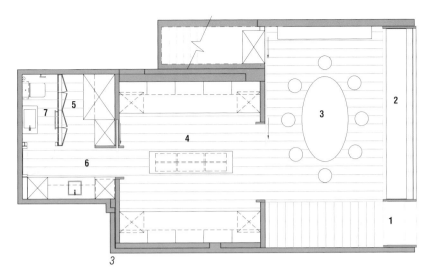

1 Entry
2 Raised platform
3 Conference room
4 Workspace
5 Printing/copier area
6 Kitchen
7 W/C

3

4

Bishop's See South Lobby

Perth, Western Australia, Australia

fitzpatrick+partners

The site of this commercial office building is part of a historic precinct. The design response takes cues from the typology of a temple – a heavy flat base beneath a building that exposes its structure, allowing connections to the surrounding landscape between its structural bays. The ground floor is shared by office space facing south over the gardens, a generous open foyer and conference facilities facing north.

The concept for the lobby was to create a warm and inviting space through the use of timeless materials and finishes in parallel with the structure's honest expression. The primary floor and wall material is travertine stone. This stone has been used for centuries in public spaces, and its soft ochre colour and grain create a sense of warmth.

The wall behind the reception desk is clad in classical, onyx-marbled stone, which is partly translucent. This, combined with the figuring and clouding of the stone, gives a visual depth to the panels and creates a feature wall – the optimum location for building signage. Wall corners are detailed with projecting stainless steel blades, mimicked on the frames of the lift-car entries to protect the stone from damage.

The external glass walls are kept clean with minimal framing, so that they visually 'disappear' and make entering the lobby space as simple as possible. As such, frames are recessed into the floor and ceiling, with glass fins in lieu of a traditional aluminium frame. Ceiling finishes continue from inside to outside to again blur the line of enclosure.

The building's design has been awarded a 5 Green Star rating by the Green Building Council of Australia for incorporating environmental sustainable technology and amenity.

1

2

1 Café in lobby
2 Lift lobby
3 Café and seating area in lobby

Photography: Craig Kinder

3

bmf Advertising

Sydney, New South Wales, Australia
Siren Design Group

The rapid growth of advertising agency bmf called for larger premises that not only reflected its creative image to clients, but also to provide a functional and inspirational environment for its staff. The brief was to provide a vibrant, distinctive and edgy design that is on the cutting edge of creativity. The back-of-house space needed to be open plan, but it was important to have separate meeting areas from the working areas.

The reception area incorporates a curved, textured front desk, eclectic furniture and recycled French wrought-iron gates framed by timber columns that lead through to the games room where racing car simulators and pinball machines invite clients and staff to have fun. The client meeting rooms next to the reception area are inviting and stimulating, each with its own character echoing the company's diversity. The addition of a mezzanine level to the back area enabled the designers to plan bench-style desks among the ceiling trusses. The open-plan work areas house large workstations with custom-designed 'crash mat' visitor seating encouraging creativity and fun. The use of oversized graphic feature walls and bold colours throughout the fitout help invigorate the space.

The aim of the project was to enhance the spirit of the iconic Festival Records Building, a pre-war art deco classic, by mixing the old with the new and ensuring that the heritage features of the infamous building were respected and showcased. The use of recycled materials sourced from various sites, including timber columns, existing feature tiling and parquetry flooring, has revived the historical building. Existing lounges were re-upholstered, task chairs were reused and meeting room tables were re-figured to suit the new space and bmf's requirements.

1

1 Forest imagery lines the meeting room corridors

2 Meeting rooms mix glass, steel and timber, creating private spaces

3 Eclectic furniture and lighting feature in the reception area

Photography: Brendan Read Photography

2

3

Boy Scouts of America, Orange County Council Headquarters

Santa Ana, California, USA

MVE & Partners

The architect's design solution for the Boy Scouts of America, Orange County Council was to use common building materials in a creative manner, resulting in a space that visually expresses the resourcefulness and ingenuity at the heart of scouting.

Beyond the single-storey glass doors, a fireplace is set within the wall to the left of the entryway, under a one-metre-high logo made of oxidised copper that was formerly located on the exterior of the original headquarters building. Across the wood-grain vinyl flooring, white lettering spans the length of the open lobby to read the famous motto: 'Be Prepared', while leading to the reception desk at the centre.

On the first floor, the retail store features exposed rafters, air shafts and piping at the ceiling level. The flooring is mainly carpet, except for a wavy hardwood path through the centre of the store. Mirroring the path at the ceiling is a series of stretched fabric shapes that – coupled with the flooring pattern – act as a strong directional device.

The main floor also houses conference rooms of multiple sizes, restrooms, an elevator and a flight of stairs leading to the second floor. Alongside the staircase is a concrete, larger-than-life-size statue of a Boy Scout in uniform.

Housed on the second floor is a large cubicle office area where specific sections are separated by wooden folding dividers with large black-and-white photos of Boy Scout troops. This photography detailing is part of the custom-designed graphics program created by the MVE & Partners in-house graphic design team. The program incorporates directional signage, donor plaques and honour walls, along with the vintage photographs and a 14-metre mural spelling out the Boy Scouts pledge. The material palette is consistent throughout, punctuated with splashes of colour on select walls and furniture.

1

2

3

4

5

1 Boy Scouts' emblem glows from within a glass-block tower

2 The famous motto welcomes visitors in the reception area

3 Stairs within the glass-block tower lead to offices

4 Large-scale photos of scouting weave the organisation's history through the space

5 A wood-grained path guides shoppers through the Scout store

Photography: Lawrence Anderson

CHC Studio

Melbourne, Victoria, Australia

ClarkeHopkinsClarke

1

The new ClarkeHopkinsClarke Studio creates a work environment that challenges the traditional office. It blurs the boundaries between indoor and outdoor space, creates a tension between street and studio and between light and dark elements, and provides a working environment that supports creativity, productivity and community.

The studio is indicative of the continuing evolution of the formerly semi-industrial area. The large glazed street elevation reflects the heritage warehouses opposite and provides glimpses of the activity within. The refined rectilinear form of the studio is informed by the industrial character of the surrounding streets and is enlivened by the addition of the curved boardroom, projecting over the entry to the carpark.

The planning emphasises the importance of collaboration and teamwork. A large entrance and reception area welcomes visitors and provides a place for informal gatherings. Key spaces for meeting with clients and consultant teams are located at the front of the building so that they are accessible and visible. The main studio space is located half a level above the foyer and wraps around a central courtyard and staff room, bringing light, air and life into the work environment.

A simple and rational construction methodology was used to reduce the need for complicated systems and construction. The design celebrates the character and qualities of the selected materials in their natural form with clear and simple detailing.

The new studio is a built example of the firm's commitment to environmentally sustainable design. The practical application of passive and active ESD principles and technologies has created a light-filled, temperate and healthy work environment.

2

3

4

1 Entrance

2 Workspace around the courtyard

3 View from the courtyard into the
  lunch room

4 Reception foyer

Photography: Rhiannon Slatter

COFRA/Good Energies North American Headquarters Offices

New York, New York, USA

Perkins + Will

The new COFRA Group offices combine spaces for five separate companies. While all operate under the Swiss parent company's mantra of environmental and social responsibility, each had varying workstyles and ideas about the new office space.

The project brief called for the highest level of sustainable design, but the design team needed to balance that with the client's non-negotiable request for private, perimeter offices. The resulting design is an innovative response to those conflicting requirements, balancing private offices with expansive openness, views and daylight from every point on the floor. The design includes the incorporation of sustainable products in which Good Energies invests – both for symbolic and marketing purposes.

The space features daylight and expansive Manhattan views from nearly every viewpoint on the floor. The boardroom, which features custom modular tables, can flex from one large room or two smaller ones when needed. Graphics throughout the glass-filled space convey identity, unity and varying levels of privacy. In many aspects, the project exceeds requirements for its LEED-CI Gold rating. Water exceeds LEED reduction requirements by 25 percent, a commitment to ongoing 100-percent green power far surpasses the required two years, 98 percent of FSC-certified wood is twice the amount required, and 42 percent of materials are locally manufactured. All insulation is made from recycled denim jeans, 80 percent of construction waste was diverted from landfill and 22 percent of the total materials are recycled content. A green housekeeping plan, educational signage, occupancy sensors and daylight harvesting ensure that the employees are reminded of the green mission well into the future. The space also functions as a marketing tool, featuring the products in which Good Energies invests.

1   Conference room
2   Central pantry area with views to windows
3   Private office with LED lights and daylight sensors
4   View from elevator lobby

Photography: Eduard Hueber/ArchPhoto

1

2

3

4

Confucius Institute

Brisbane, Queensland, Australia

Suters Architects

The 150-square-metre Confucius Institute consists of a generous entry and reception area, a meeting room with kitchen facilities, a utility area, an open workstation area and two offices.

The facility was commissioned by Queensland University of Technology for the Confucius Institute – an organisation set up to develop cultural awareness and understanding and to teach the Chinese language in universities outside China. The architect developed the conceptual framework strategy around the idea of a Chinese lantern. The lantern shapes the space as a beacon of light within the sombre encompassing fabric of its existing environment – a space within a space.

The architect created an outer shell of CFC panels to contrast against the surrounding faced blockwork walls of the adjacent building and to define the envelope. Generous entry glazing and deep window reveals direct the eye to key points within the interior of the lit space.

Internal walls were kept off the external envelope to emphasise the 'space within a space' quality the architect identified within the conceptual framework. White walls and joinery contrast with the dark bamboo flooring and reception countertop. Splashes of red within seating, tile splashback and the display cabinet subtly allude to the building's cultural purpose.

Key successes within the project were the revitalisation of the existing building fabric and also of the adjacent previously unused courtyard space. The architect's attention to the spaces outside the original scope of work inspired the client to redevelop surrounding garden beds to complete the project.

1

1 A space within a space
2 Reception
3 Informal landing
4 Reception and flexible activity zone

Photography: Christopher Frederick Jones

2

3

4

Edmunds.com Headquarters

Santa Monica, California, USA
STUDIOS Architecture

This 8300-square-metre headquarters office for a leading online car-buying guide and information centre functions as an urban campus with 350 employees spread over three floors linked by a central connecting stair.

The overall concept for the space was to harness the energy of the Edmunds team, and create a facility that promotes the flow of information, people and communication at each and every juncture. Like a racetrack with banked turns to allow for faster speeds, the space embodies the essence of the firm's web portal – easy to navigate and intuitive to use.

The design is inspired by the creation of motion, much like the streaks of light from passing cars speeding along a busy highway. The inspiration for the design was derived from the automotive form, Sunset Boulevard and photos of highways at dusk. The colour choices came directly from the automotive industry, incorporating Ferrari Red, Lamborghini Orange, Ford Aqua and Mercedes Silver, and other elements such as tail lights and white racing stripes. Colour was extremely important for the overall character and helped to create fluidity throughout the space, such as the strategically placed racing stripes that appear to be 'racing' one another.

The open-plan and non-hierarchical workspace fosters interaction and collegiality – not even the CEO has a private office. The space includes multiple break areas, a games room, and formal and informal meeting areas concentrated around the 'Great Room', which serves as the central assembly place for weekly all-staff meetings and special events, as well as for intimate gatherings of two or three people.

1 Connecting stair

2 Custom-designed 'skidmark' couch

3 Open-plan workspace and collaboration zone

4 Banquet seating branded with Edmunds' founding year

1

2

3

4

6

5   Informal meeting area

6   Conference room

7   Elevator lobby

8   One of several break areas

Photography: © Benny Chan/Fotoworks

7

8

Elwood Clothing Head Office

Melbourne, Victoria, Australia

matt gibson a+d

This 400-square-metre office fitout for a jeans and street-wear retailer was an exercise in combining a new workplace and brand recognition with the recycling of building stock. The company's motto of 'Tomorrow's Vintage' was a perfect fit with the 'retain/re-use/recycle' design philosophy. The brief required not only an aesthetic response, but a strategy of assimilation with the existing building – one that would become a market symbol for the Elwood identity.

The material detailing strategy was to reveal the raw, gritty industrial aesthetic of the existing building. A simple palette of natural materials (exposed brick and concrete and salvaged messmate floorboards) and colours mostly limited to black and white (white plaster, black steel and anthracite carpet) meant the interior reflected the client's passion for vintage and collector culture without overpowering the clothing.

The messmate recycled timber flooring was utilised in all the public areas as a hero statement. A 1.2- by 4-metre, 400-kilogram front entry door clad in messmate leads the visitor up the stairs to the reception landing where the same material continues to wrap around to become a large sculpted reception desk and storage unit.

Cost-effective industrial lighting in the reception area and within the stair highlights the texture of the brick feature wall and collectable items including a Benelli motorcycle and 1950s lifestyle prints. A warm linear strip light also provides a vertical link between the street entry and reception.

The exterior was partly repainted to complement its gritty nature, while external paraphernalia such as old signage letters were retained. The client did not require a sign to announce its new office; rather, the look and feel of the building reflect its culture and signify the brand.

1

2

1 The muddy, dark exterior complements the 4-metre-high recycled-timber entry door and industrial aesthetic of the interior

2 A vertical stairway of recycled timber connects the street-entry door with reception desk

3 Recycled timber reception desk symbolises Elwood Clothing's motto of 'Tomorrow's Vintage'

3

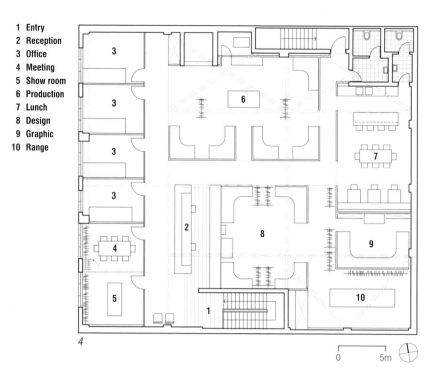

1 Entry
2 Reception
3 Office
4 Meeting
5 Show room
6 Production
7 Lunch
8 Design
9 Graphic
10 Range

0   5m

4

5

6

4   The layout promoted an inclusive and collaborative environment with the entire office being visually permeable

5   Low-rise partitioning demarcates the production, design and graphics areas; the overall feeling is of space, light and transparency

6   The interior spaces are true to the brand – simple, resourceful and elegant

Photography: Shannon McGrath

Fama Consulting Office

Mestre, Venice, Italy

Filippo Caprioglio
Caprioglio Associati
Studio di Architettura

Given that the existing space was extremely narrow, with three wall elements fragmenting the area, the design for this 90-square-metre office interior presented the architect with a challenging task. The client's requirements – an open reception, a conference room and private offices – were realised via a system of fluid curves that generate a completely new perception and experience of the space.

Complementing the new spatial configuration is the use of natural and artificial light: the former assists with understanding the complexity of the space, the latter defines the curvilinear rooms. These rooms seem to disappear inside the false ceiling troughs via a series of cylindrical spots that set the rhythm of the walls and mark the entrance to each office.

In response to the narrow space available, the conference room, which is set at the very end of the space, is treated as a transparent box that glows when in use.

1   *Reception desk*

2   *Entrance view and waiting area*

3   *External view of the conference room*

Photography: Paolo Monello

1

2

Global Management Consulting Firm

Houston, Texas, USA

Rottet Studio

This global management consulting firm desired a modular, flexible workplace in accordance with the company's core values of teamwork and collaboration of practices. Key to the design aesthetics is the connection of the reception and main gathering areas in relation to the elevator lobby. This was accomplished by using identical species figured wood elements throughout.

In the reception area, the wood element was used to the rear of the reception desk to enhance and articulate the primary entry. A comfortable waiting area facing the main glass-enclosed conference room provides an inspiring office environment for both employees and clients. At the stairs, the wood element was vertically accentuated with stainless-steel inlaid reveals aligning with the treads of the centralised staircase. The volume housing the two-storey staircase captures natural light and emphasises overall spaciousness.

Establishing common areas for informal and formal gathering is integral to the overall design approach. The large open area just off the elevator lobby is used as a flexible entertaining area that can be readily rearranged with casual furniture layouts or in a cafeteria configuration. This area can also be transformed into a training room by employing movable partitions. Nearby, the firm's lounge area with a wood-clad ceiling, located opposite the central staircase and facing a magnificent view of the city skyline, is intended as an informal congregation spot for meetings, staff celebrations or just as a relaxation area for enjoying a cup of coffee with a newspaper. The design also incorporates the firm's sophisticated art collection, which has been strategically positioned and thoughtfully lit.

To enhance the firm's team approach and collaborative interaction, several different-sized team rooms were located at the corners of the building as well as between office suites. This distribution enhances conference room accessibility and further facilitates team collaboration.

A project of Lauren Rottet while with DMJM Rottet.

1

1 Reception area

2 Staircase

3 Break room

4 Office corridor

5 West elevator lobby at night

Photography: Joe Aker – Aker/Zvonkovic Photography

2

3

4

5

Hambly and Woolley Studio

Toronto, Ontario, Canada
Cindy Rendely Architexture

The objective was to create a modest but elegant office for a boutique art and graphic design studio that would reflect and enhance the firm's reputation for creating clear, thoughtful and lighthearted work. The architect met this brief by defining the interior with colour and flaunting a minimal palette of inexpensive materials. In particular, recycled wood was treated in an unusual fashion to reflect the firm's eco-awareness, creativity and its ability to do a lot with a little.

The 370-square-metre studio office is situated on the top floor of a historic warehouse building in downtown Toronto, with limited access to natural light due to surrounding buildings on three sides. Limited to only essential elements, the aim was to give all millwork, furnishing, light fixtures, doors and windows a sculptural appearance and to establish a blank backdrop for the studio's own work and its collection of globes.

The space was stripped to its essential elements, exposing ductwork and timber floors, ceilings and beams. Perimeter offices were created and punctured with frosted windows at playful heights, allowing natural light to penetrate into the heart of the floor and affording a sense of intrigue and visual openness.

A reduced palette of inexpensive materials – paint, laminate and reclaimed wood – define the interior's warm and casual aesthetic and imbue the space with a graphic quality. The unusual hues of the colour-splashed walls were drawn from the firm's logo. Patchwork wood millwork, tabletops and doors were simply varnished to expose their natural beauty, complementing the building's original features. Inward-looking and calmly detailed, the office's unity and compositional clarity is derived from good proportions, intuitive circulation and adjacencies, with a blurring of plinth, edge, wall and furniture.

1

1 Reception
2 Central layout space

3

4

5

3 Meeting room

4 Staff kitchen

5 Layout area with view to pin-up wall

Photography: Tom Arban

Hatch Associates

Brisbane, Queensland, Australia

Hassell

The new workplace of worldwide engineering firm Hatch Associates is in a heritage precinct of Brisbane. The design reflects the results of a detailed briefing developed with Hatch staff. A series of surveys, interviews and workshops set functional and aspirational goals and captured company culture and brand values, represented in the design of the workplace.

The workplace comprises office space in the historic Petrie Barracks building and a new separate four-level building. The design responds to the heritage constraints of the existing Barracks building and the dynamics of a new commercial office building. It provides diverse and adaptable arrangements that allow for flexibility in how and where staff interact and work.

The large floor plates of the development posed a challenge in defining the boundaries of the space. The articulated central nodes are a mechanism for defining zones, creating social and working neighbourhoods within the large building footprint. Diagrams articulating circulation, daylight penetration and noisy versus quiet spaces confirmed the hierarchy and adjacency of spaces from this centre node. The hubs are a collaborative heart connecting the workspace through the use of internal voids and external stairs.

1

2

1 The workplace reception
2 Meeting area circulation space
3 Waiting area for staff and clients

4

5

6

4   Executive carrels for concentrated work

5   Recycled timber wall in reception

6   Staff hubs linked by void

7   Workplace floor plan

8   Graphics infuse colour

Photography: Christopher Frederick Jones

7

8

Haus im Haus

Hamburg, Germany

Behnisch Architekten

Hamburg's Chamber of Commerce, a hub of the city's economic life, required a more intensive use of its existing neo-classical building in the city centre. The architects' brief anticipated the introduction of additional floor levels within the existing 'Börsenhalle' and a structure that respects the fabric of the historic building.

In consideration of both the structural condition of the listed Börsenhalle and the mandatory preservation of its historical features, a new five-storey structure was inserted into it: a 'house within a house' that comprises approximately 1000 square metres for new usages and also reflects, in contemporary style, the building's long history as a meeting point of Hamburg's business communities.

The new structure occupies a relatively small proportion of the hall in order to preserve its generous spatial character. A business start-up centre, consultation, exhibition, club and meeting room facilities are arranged in a sculptural manner. The uppermost level affords access to generous roof terraces. The structure is composed of layers and planes, where lightness, immateriality and reflection contrast with the solid, elaborate walls of the existing building. It unfolds as seemingly free-floating levels and planes that consciously contrast with the historic hall's ponderous stone bulk: the soft lines of vaulted constructions juxtaposed with the clear lines of the new structure, a bright apparition constructed of luminous, transparent and reflective materials, reminiscent of a glittering, multi-faceted jewel that absorbs and refracts light.

The new extension functions as a prism through which the historic hall can be perceived from various perspectives in unendingly new variations. The light, free-floating character of the new extension is complemented and accentuated by a LED lighting system that was jointly developed by the architects and Nimbus Design. A challenge of this project was to not simply light the building, but to use light to make the building appear to float.

1   *The new 'house in a house' in the listed former stock exchange building*

2   *Cantilevered main stair*

3   *Bridge to Albert Schäfer Auditorium*

1

2

3

4

5

6

7

4 Level 1: view into the business start-up centre

5 Exhibition area

6 Level 2: bridge to Albert Schäfer Auditorium with view of the exhibition area

7 Level 4: restaurant and Börsen Club

8 Level 4: bar in restaurant

9 Börsen Club cabinets

Photography: Hans Jürgen Landes

8

9

Lime Rock Partners

Houston, Texas, USA

Rottet Studio

This energy investment firm charged the designers with creating a dynamic environment that distinguished and supported the firm's two operating teams, while establishing common areas for meetings and entertainment. The building's unusual structural design and a desire to capture the downtown views greatly influenced space planning.

Two floating glass boxes were created within the interior floor plan to house individual offices. The boxes are defined by folding planes of colour, wood, art and glass strategically placed on one-third of each office, allowing natural light to penetrate the interior while maintaining privacy. The distinction between floor, wall, ceiling and furniture becomes blurred as the materials wrap and fold to create these surfaces.

The environment uses design elements to identify the association with the oil and gas industry. Linear patterns found in the strata of geological formations were repeated in a custom-designed rug, fabrics and an ethereal ceiling sculpture created by Houston artist Paul Fleming. While the art and graphics are bold, the materials palette used is simple and reflective. The space becomes a living work, reflective of the business and the energetic attitudes of the company.

A project of Lauren Rottet while with DMJM Rottet.

1

1 Formal reception

2 Entry

3 Formal conference room

4 Principal's office

5 Informal reception

Photography: Benny Chan, Fotoworks

2

3

4

5

Liquidnet

New York, New York, USA

STUDIOS Architecture

Liquidnet's global headquarters occupies 3000 square metres spread over five floors of a former garment factory building in midtown Manhattan. The goal was to create a space that represents the ethos of this customer-focused global institutional marketplace headquarters. Most important to the client was to show how its business functions through openness and collaboration. Visitors see staff members meeting and eating together, demonstrating that the space – and the company – is a place for collaboration.

Just beyond the front desk, an internal, glass-enclosed connecting staircase anchors the central circulation hub and provides quick, efficient access between the principal three floors. An open commons with a café surrounds this central staircase and is utilised as a waiting area for guests, an informal meeting and gathering area for employees and visitors and a presentation event space. Natural light streams through glass walls that provide acoustic privacy for three adjacent conference and meeting rooms with exterior windows. The use of SwitchLite Privacy Glass™ provides visual privacy for these conference rooms when needed. An oversized rear-projection wall is used for product demonstrations as well as a digital bulletin board for company announcements.

Work areas surround the central reception area and commons. Offices for senior management are glass enclosed and located along the perimeter of open work areas used by the marketing, sales and customer service departments. Custom modular workstations were developed to provide increased communication, unobstructed visual access and flexibility to adapt to future growth and change. Server power wiring for the workstations is displayed neatly in power and data glass riser cabinets to reiterate the theme of transparency.

1

1 Glass-enclosed stair
2 Seating area in commons with conference room beyond

3

3 Commons space

4 Workspace

5 Internal stair

6 Seating area within commons

Photography: Eric Laignel

4

5

6

Lloyd's Reinsurance Company (China) Ltd

Shanghai, China

M Moser Associates

For its planned entry into China, Lloyd's required a workspace that would dramatise its ethos and centuries-old reputation for integrity and innovation. This objective was accomplished by creating an office design of simplicity and transparency. The result was a 750-square-metre space of high-tech functionality and aesthetically pleasing lines.

Achieving the clean appearance of the space was a design challenge, because of the necessity for total concealment of the sophisticated communication technologies that Lloyd's relies on for its business. M Moser Technology, the technology and engineering division of the M Moser group, achieved a genuinely paper-free office by secreting all wiring and AV equipment inside walls and floors. In addition, the conference room table has high-tech elements for telecommunication purposes, but there are no visible pieces of equipment in the room.

The impressive end result of this effort is a minimalist environment whose Spartan simplicity perfectly mirrors the professional, open and transparent manner in which Lloyd's and its underwriters manage risk.

Additionally, high levels of privacy and autonomy were created by providing an independent workspace for each underwriting syndicate. The ingenious use of semi-closed glass partitions to link syndicates to both their neighbours and the outside world helped to add to the overall feeling of openness and transparency.

The workspace also needed to reflect Lloyd's commitment to China in a credible yet understated way. Rather than use super-graphics, which would have detracted from the office's overall minimalism, the spectacular views of Shanghai available through Lloyd's 33rd floor windows provided the visual backdrop. Staff and visitors are surrounded by a living wallpaper that changes as the city itself changes. With views of the Bund and the Pearl Tower representing Shanghai's past and present, respectively, Lloyd's itself becomes the gateway to Shanghai's future.

1

2

3

1 The utmost care has been taken to ensure the space is clean and uncluttered

2 A window-side lounge channels end-to-end visibility

3 Reflections increase the depth of the space

4 Curved glass partitioning smoothes the transition between public areas and syndicate workspace

Photography: Vitus Lau

4

Meerkin & Apel Lawyers

Melbourne, Victoria, Australia

Inarc Architects

The client's brief was for an environment that challenged the standard model of overly refined office accommodation, something that would set them apart from similar businesses. The architect's task was to fashion a suitable environment out of a number of disparate building elements including a Victorian two-storey terrace house and a number of ageing early-20th-century factory buildings to the rear.

At the ground level there is extensive off-street parking at the rear and reception via the shop front. The three-level top-lit stair void leads up to the main office floor. The main office area is a vast double-height space reminiscent of a banking chamber. Within this space a mezzanine floor overlooks the main office floor and includes a staff café and library. The top floor has been dedicated to conference and meeting rooms with expansive skyline views.

The commercial budget was a major factor in decisions regarding building systems, materials and interior detailing and finishes. An industrial aesthetic was adopted for both the structure and the interiors, leaving structure and services exposed and reducing the amount of finishing required.

Existing building elements were retained where possible. The new construction utilises honed-concrete slab floors, second-hand brick walls, recycled timber flooring and panels of hoop pine-veneered plywood. The soft south light throughout the building gives the building a feeling of a vast industrial gallery rather than that of an office.

The orientation of the building minimises heat gain and the bulk of areas with double-glazing are oriented to the south. An atrium acts as a passive heat and ventilation stack with openings at the top level to enable hot air to escape. The luxury of space and lofty ceiling heights are a departure from the office norm.

1

1 View of main reception, ground floor

2 View of conference room facility on the top floor

3   *Level 2 floor plan*

4   *Waiting area in base of atrium*

5   *View from managing director's suite into atrium on level 2*

6   *Stair in central atrium on level 2*

7   *Bridge across atrium at top-level conference facility*

8   *Mezzanine staff break-out area and library overlooking general office on level 2*

Photography: Peter Clarke, Latitude

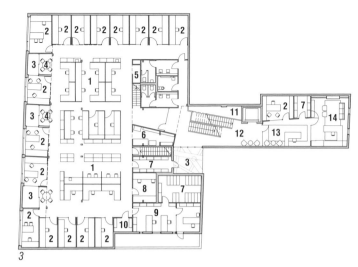

1   **Open workspace**
2   **Office**
3   **Terrace**
4   **Breakout space**
5   **Cloak room**
6   **Print room**
7   **Filing**
8   **Systems administration**
9   **Accounts**
10   **Store**
11   **Void**
12   **Atrium**
13   **Waiting area**
14   **Director's office**

3

4

5

6

7

8

Middletons

Melbourne, Victoria, Australia

Gray Puksand

For this CBD office interior, the architects were inspired by the work of artists who have utilised a minimalist vocabulary to create expressions that can translate to the world of interior design. The refit of this commercial law firm office takes its cues from such erudite experiments in the expression of space, form and sculpture as practised by artists including James Turrell, Dan Flavin and Donald Judd. The palette of design elements has been deliberately pared down to the essentials: the use of light and space as physical design elements has driven the interior design solution.

The project relies on contemporary materials and techniques to achieve the design result. Computer-driven laser cutting and routing was used to create the dominant reception feature screens; thin-profile LED lighting was used in general signage and to create the illuminated room numbering on the reception level; stainless steel chainwire mesh was digitally reproduced within the film pattern to meeting rooms; and Corian was used extensively to create jointless joinery units.

Space planning maximised daylight quality and access, reducing the use of artificial lighting. Individual switches minimise usage and increase flexibility so lights can be used only when needed.

Maximising energy efficiency and indoor environment quality were priorities. Low-VOC materials included Marmoleum linoleum used in conjunction with low-solvent Forbo Fix adhesive; Echopanel, a 100-percent recyclable PET product, used for pin boards in tearooms and workstation screens; and Ultima acoustic ceiling tile system, with 66–78 percent recycled content used in video conference room ceilings.

1 'Front door'
2 Reception

1

3

4

3 Public face – reception

4 Breakout area

5 Client floor plan

6 Client floor

7 Client floor – meeting room detail

Photography: Peter Clarke, Latitude

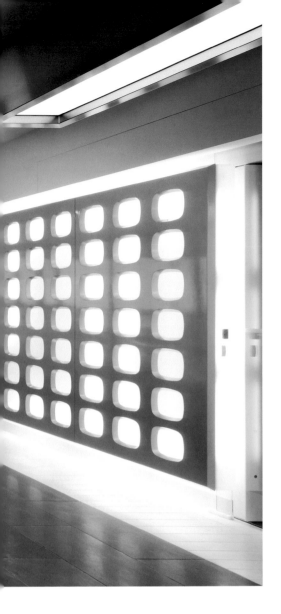

5

6

7

National Foods

Melbourne Docklands, Victoria, Australia

Hassell

The new National Foods workplace reflects the aspiration of this food production enterprise to remain connected to the land and in touch with the people involved in the process of creating food. A desire to use the workplace to reinforce a market-leading position and celebrate the vitality of the firm's various brands is embedded in the interior design.

The interior of the building was carefully designed to bring staff and products together, both literally and figuratively. Metaphors are used throughout the workplace to subtly reinforce the company's commitment to its people and brands.

A six-storey spiral staircase is a metaphor for pouring milk, and also a key device in maintaining collaboration between staff on different levels. Sculptural plant walls signal a connection with nature, but also assist in improving indoor air quality and enhancing staff wellbeing. The reception area is visually linked to a testing kitchen, giving visitors the opportunity to observe food being prepared and tested.

The design takes a non-traditional approach to corporate environments and acknowledges the journey of ingredients from farm to factory. It celebrates and reinforces National Foods' commitment to primary producers, manufacturing and food production.

1

1   Vertical circulation is connected to staff hub

2   Reception lounge

3   Staff hub

4   Active informal meeting area

5   The six-storey spiral staircase

Photography: Shannon McGrath

2

3

4

5

Nokia Headquarters

Beijing, China

M Moser Associates

1

Nokia set up its China headquarters in a newly developed area in Beijing to house its R&D and business units, which were previously dispersed around Beijing. The project resulted in a six-floor, 80,000-square-metre campus that enables better collaboration across operations as well as adjacency to its supply chain.

The facility was designed using an inside-out approach, with the interior needs being considered first and then the exterior architecture being built to allow for these requirements. Needs were assessed through end-user engagement, which also served to gain buy-in with stakeholders.

The campus had to cater for potential changes and also enable future growth. Because of the building's modular design approach, changes that occurred were easily integrated into the design. The design also enabled flexibility in working style for staff. Staff were able to choose from a variety of shared and private spaces that included formal and informal meeting spaces, private phone booths and break-out spaces. Staff were also able to choose where they work through a mobile working concept.

Because the new headquarters is an hour from the Beijing city centre, with very limited services and amenities, offices were grouped around a Main Street that created a 'mini-township' feeling. This township provided people an opportunity to meet and collaborate across different operations, while taking advantage of the services and amenities that helped balance staff life/work needs. Some of these added-value places included restaurants, a convenience store, banking facilities, a spa and even a jet-lag room. Unique services provided include personal trainers, concierge and health services.

Another major design consideration was sustainability. Quantifiable achievements in energy savings, reuse and recycling of materials, natural lighting conditions and a high-quality indoor air environment led to the Nokia facility being the first corporate building in China to achieve LEED Gold certification.

2

1 The mini-township as seen in the sunlit full-height atrium

2 The project includes a variety of restaurants with international cuisines

3 Areas adjacent to the main street include formal and informal meeting spaces

4 R&D and business units are connected by lift lobbies on both ends

5 Meeting rooms are plentiful and diverse in plan

Photography: Vitus Lau

3

4

5

NORTH Advertising

Portland, Oregon, USA

Skylab Architecture

NORTH is a branding agency that was seeking a new kind of office structure to encourage collaborative thinking and fresh ideas.

Based on the idea of a polar research expedition to the frontier, a 1000-square-metre 'basecamp' was designed. The design responds to alternative social interactions – cooking, eating, lounging and gaming – that inspire creative work. Workstations are replaced with modular structures, furniture and equipment defined around activity. Collaboration is based on portability and a cluster-on-demand breakaway from the traditional static office.

The building, formerly home to a printing business, is on the National Register of Historic Places. The basecamp tent – the historic building shell – was left untouched. Interior walls and structures are not fixed to the shell. Pine panelling, raw steel and a carpet tile mural on the floor are the predominant interior features. Floral drapery and camouflage 'Fatboy' beanbags allow for reflecting 'around a campfire'.

A cantilevered 'think' module is vertically stacked in the centre of the space. A series of interspersed glass and metal panels define the edit module, two soundproof rooms without doors. Smoke plush carpeting and mirror-like edit stations make editing a destination without wasting carbon.

Taking a universal icon for quick creative thought and communication, the media module is Post-it Note yellow. A commercial-grade kitchen and adjacent dining area with picnic tables, wall mural and topographic carpet tiles redefines the outdoors inside. A visitor module of smoke walls and ice-white lighting is curated with print, sound and new media inspirations, fostering an ever-changing creative forum and a connection with the local community.

1   *A renewed historic building and former printing business, the building shell was left untouched*
2   *Cooking, eating, lounging and gaming inspire creative work and are integral to the design*
3   *A visitor module is regularly curated with print, sound and new media inspirations*
4   *A 'think module' conference room reveals elevated views through clerestory windows*

Photography: Jeremy Bittermann

1

2

3

4

Paul, Hastings, Janofsky & Walker, LLP

New York, New York, USA

Rottet Studio

Paul, Hastings, Janofsky & Walker, a multidisciplinary law firm with offices worldwide, desired a unifying design scheme for its offices to reinforce its corporate identity and branding efforts and to reflect the culture of a dynamic law firm.

The new design reflects Paul Hastings' creative and forward-thinking philosophy and its image as a leading international law firm. The new workspaces, incorporating cutting-edge technology, help the firm work smarter and more efficiently.

For its New York offices, Paul Hastings chose to consolidate its two prior New York locations into a single office on 11 consecutive floors in a Helmut Jahn-designed high-rise in Midtown Manhattan. The floor plate of the new building was unusual with its non-central core, irregular angled corners and non-uniform column spacing. Consequently, the design team chose to arrange the floor plan with support spaces – a conference room, files and pantry – in the centre and private offices lining the perimeter. Anchoring the project is an interconnecting staircase linking the conference centre with all eight typical attorney floors above.

Additional architectural features include a double-height atrium space in the main reception, a series of forced-perspective corridors, dropped drywall soffits and tapered walls. All of these devices enhance the theme of 'endless space', making the interiors look and feel larger than their physical space.

Glass doors, walls and counter surfaces are used to reflect and emit light throughout the project. Along with white angled walls and undetectable mirrors, they help extend the space. Custom-designed workstations for administrative support play an integral role in the design concept.

This project received a Merit Award from the American Institute of Architects Houston Chapter and a coveted Solutia Doc Award for Design Excellence.

A project of Lauren Rottet while with DMJM Rottet.

1

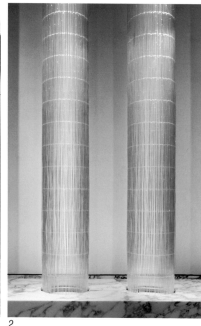

2

1 Elevator detail

2 Reception art

3 Reception

Photography: Michael Moran

3

Registrar-Recorder/County Clerk Elections Operations Center

Santa Fe Springs, California, USA

Lehrer Architects

This project was about housing the infrastructure of democracy, as the people who work here handle, prepare and maintain the balloting equipment and materials used in every voting station throughout Los Angeles County. The architects tackled this design project by transforming the original, awkward, over-budget plan to create an efficient, streamlined work place. The architects considered colour, size, placement and basic proportions in configuring a space that effected a positive change in how employees work.

The warehouse presented an opportunity to implement bright, bold colours, which proved to be a thrifty way of making large-scale change in the space. Bright reds, oranges and greens energise the entire area, including the 3.5-metre-high divider walls placed in different areas of the warehouse. A bright red wall leads into the space beyond the entrance and the offices that front the building.

A critical architectural move was the use of mega-banner technology to provide scale and intimacy to the huge warehouse. The architect envisioned large-scale banners that could display symbols or imagery. The clients worked with the Los Angeles County Arts Commission and the One Percent for Art Program to commission a local artist, UCLA professor, Rebeca Mendez. Mendez created a 4.5- by 40-metre hanging banner titled *Tree by Tree, from Sea to Mountains*, 2008 – a panoramic sequence of photographs that runs from the Pacific Ocean to the San Gabriel Mountains, showing trees, water and sky, and affords the cavernous space a more intimate atmosphere. A set of nine nature-themed vertical banners were placed at the ends of the 9- by 60-metre stacks, creating the 'room' in which most warehouse workers spend their day.

1

1   *The huge banner mitigates the cavernous space and lets nature in*

2   *Storage stacks are delineated vertically by photo banners and horizontally by broad orange stripes*

3   *Colourful stripes and solids enliven and add form to the large warehouse*

4   *Stripes – as a recurring graphic – suggest a subtle American flag motif*

Photography: Lehrer Architects

2

3

4

RMIT Student Union

Melbourne, Victoria, Australia

I:I Architects

The Royal Melbourne Institute of Technology's city campus, located in the heart of Melbourne's CBD, houses many of the university's key functions. The Student Union premises, located on a major city thoroughfare, required a total upgrade of the existing architectural and building services.

The brief for the fitout was to create a vibrant hub for the student union body that would transform the area from the former defunct union shop with associated offices to a dedicated space to cater for the various student union activities. The design accommodates a front of house area, a mix of open-plan and enclosed offices, kitchen, copying, lounge and library facilities.

The interface of the Student Union is articulated by stained plywood walls and glazed infill panels that create visual connection between the public corridor and the Student Union area. The existing glass brickwork located along the perimeter of the building was retained and provided the source of inspiration for adaptation of the pixel motif as a design element throughout the fitout. The pixel motif inspired the design of the joinery shelving, the pattern to the stained plywood walls, the internal windows and the film patterns to the office glazing.

The main open workstation area has an exposed concrete soffit ceiling, expressing the service pipes, air-conditioning ducts, cables and inner workings of the building. Painted black, the ceiling provides a backdrop to the suspended timber acoustic panels that float over the workstations. A neutral palette and use of natural timbers offsets the strength of the dark ceiling and together they complement the sharpness of the white workstations.

1   View of the main corridor

2   Kitchen and open office area

3   Shelving and workstation area

4   Workstation

Photography: Michael Laurie

1

2

3

4

Robert Mills – Grattan Street Office

Melbourne, Victoria, Australia

Robert Mills Architect Pty Ltd

This office was strategically designed to showcase the architect's design vision of pure form and function. The clean open-plan lines and neutral finishes create an environment to inspire creativity.

The Grattan Street building was transformed from a derelict factory to a single warehouse space. The predominant features of the building are a 332-square-metre ground-floor open-plan office, reception and meeting area, and a 62-square-metre mezzanine, which functions as a as a private office and second meeting room.

Clear zones are indicated by the subtle use of partitions and low-level walls that encourage a visual flow throughout the space, while not interrupting the existing vernacular of the building.

A palette of dark timber floors, white walls and feature lighting create a neutral backdrop. Handpicked indigenous Australian artworks add colour throughout the space. Quality fittings were carefully chosen to add texture and richness, transforming the space from a factory environment to a high-end boutique-style office.

By cleverly altering the interior space and existing building fabric, features of the original architecture – such as the clerestory windows, trusses and the mezzanine level – were preserved. The natural light from the clerestory windows is drawn into the open-plan space and the mezzanine level, while the stunning 1960s terrazzo staircase was retained to link the ground and first floors. The project provided a sustainable solution that minimised energy consumption while enhancing the quality of the interior.

1

2

3

3 Library

4 Ground-floor meeting space

5 Ground floor plan

6 Mezzanine workspace overlooking the ground floor

Photography: Shannon McGrath

4

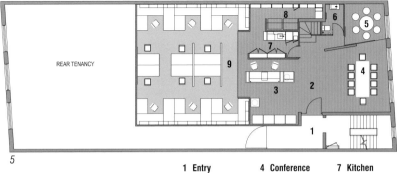

5

1	Entry	4	Conference	7	Kitchen
2	Waiting room	5	Meeting room	8	Print room
3	Reception	6	Toilet	9	General office

6

SOHO China Corporate Headquarters

Beijing, China
Leigh & Orange Ltd.

This headquarters for SOHO China, one of the country's most dynamic developers, is situated at the heart of the mixed-use Chaowai SOHO office and retail complex in Beijing.

Having previously collaborated with SOHO on a number of occasions, Leigh & Orange was given free rein to create a looser fit and less traditionally corporate-looking project.

The project comprises generous interactive spaces for ad hoc meeting, lounging, coffee and recreation amid a strict brief of departmental meeting rooms and closed and open-plan office spaces.

A meeting zone is located on the 10th floor where, after hours, this double-height space becomes the focus for social contact and interaction. The reading area and coffee bar are located above, at a junction where all staff pass, providing open views to the activities on the 10th floor. Executive offices occupy the 12th floor and provide direct connection to the roof gardens, which contain plants and water elements.

The offices have a neutral background, use natural materials and contain a diversity of plants and artworks. The stencilled metal screens at the reception area have an intriguing pattern, conceived by renowned graphic designer, Lilian Tang, and illustrate the Chinese concept of 'Chi'. By following daylight patterns, this screen casts a variety of shadows of flowing water and rock that wash over and energise the interior. To augment this, similarly patterned etched-glass division partitions and hand-woven carpet further embellish the overall internal office environment.

1   *A diversity of plants and artworks are featured*
2   *The patterned etched-glass division partitions enhance the overall internal office environment*

1

2

3

4

5

3 Open-plan office space

4 Offices have a neutral background

5 Office furnishings include the patterned hand-woven carpet

6 The graphic illustrates the Chinese concept of 'Chi'

Photography: courtesy Leigh & Orange Ltd.

6

Sorrento Science Complex (SSC)

San Diego, California, USA

McFarlane Architects, Inc.

Being new to San Diego, the client wanted to completely renovate the existing lobby and build new executive offices in order to present a better impression to visitors and attract new talent. The architects were asked to create a lobby with a sophisticated appeal and executive offices that were unique and open while providing the necessary privacy that the company's decision makers needed.

The lobby design created a sense of grandeur and elegance by raising the ceiling by means of a barrel-vaulted suspended ceiling with indirect lighting, light and dark contrasting wood panelling on the walls and reception desk, and marble flooring. The executive offices were designed with a sawtooth outline with full-height glass walls to give an open and spacious feeling, and partially covered with glazing film to provide the necessary privacy.

1

2

1 Lobby

2 Administration station

3 Administration area

Photography: Brady Architectural Photography

3

Stephen Hart Studio

Queensland, Australia

coop creative – interior design

This entire building needed upgrading, without detracting from the qualities of this traditional atelier. The materials couldn't be slick, the intervention had to develop its own patina, almost as if the artist created it himself. The client is a sculptor who creates his art in a traditional manner. His brief was a 1475 painting by Antonello Da Messina, *Saint Jerome in his Study*. The internal frames or scenes within the painting and the elevation of Saint Jerome in his study are integral to the response of the space.

A long pod of servant spaces runs the length of the studio. The pod's lower and upper shelves create a symbolic space between inner and outer worlds, referred to as 'en' space in Japanese architecture. The 'en' space implies connection and separation – the transition from the studio floor to the servant space is slowed down and the step acts as a backdrop to display finished work. The use of 'en' space suggests an ambivalent interpretation of man's being – his social structures and artefacts are seen as a part of each other.

1

2

3

4

1   Street elevation – view to workshop

2   Desk overlooking workshop

3   Workshop with office pod closed down along wall

4   Workshop viewed from kitchen pod

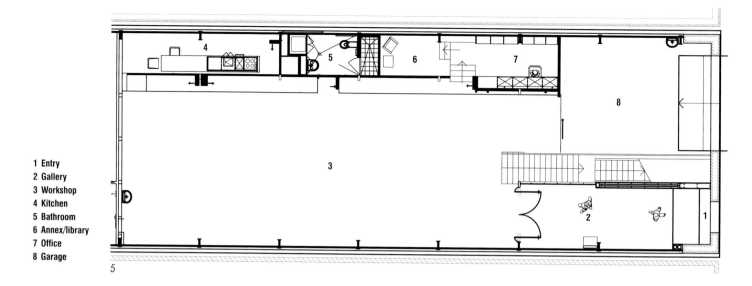

1 Entry
2 Gallery
3 Workshop
4 Kitchen
5 Bathroom
6 Annex/library
7 Office
8 Garage

5

6

7

8

5   Floor plan

6   Stephen in his workshop with kitchen behind

7   Office pod overlooks entry and workshop

8   Office

Photography: Jon Linkins

Studio Ippolito Fleitz Group

Stuttgart, Baden-Württemberg, Germany

Ippolito Fleitz Group

As a result of growth in staff numbers, the architects and communication designers of this firm worked together to create a new workplace on a single floor in an old office building. The design of the space is in accordance with the firm's own standards as 'identity architects' – the office is the hallmark that conveys its identity to both clients and staff.

Two long work desks cultivate a creative and communicative atmosphere. Shelving and furniture feature white and dark wood. Contrasting accents of colour are provided by textile bands above the work desks that serve as light switches, and from areas of green plants.

In addition to two conference rooms, cheerful communication islands are available for discussions. The studio, with its spacious kitchen and oversized mirror, is a place for inspiration and relaxation.

1

2

1 Reception desk
2 Wall system opposite the reception desk
3 Large conference room with a 'cloud' of lights
4 The small conference room has an intimate atmosphere

3

4

5

5 Textile bands above every workstation function as light switches

6 Library and a cosy communication island

Photography: Zooey Braun

Suters Head Office

Newcastle, New South Wales, Australia
Suters Architects

Requisites for this fit out for an architectural practice included functional work areas, easy interaction between staff and flexibility of use. File and drawing storage were key components and resolving how to accommodate these zones without cluttering the area was a challenge. It was decided to elevate these areas and place them above the workstations. This allowed separation of areas and also kept working files within close proximity, without compromising the historic fabric of the existing building.

Formal and informal meeting and design studio zones have been incorporated within the spaces to facilitate design group discussions and to provide spill-over spaces for formal meeting rooms. The openness of the workspace gives the office an active and functional feel without causing excessive disruption.

A large boardroom accommodating a minimum of 20 people incorporates all necessary current technologies into one integrated audiovisual multimedia system. Three additional meeting rooms are located within the reception area, one in the style of an informal lounge. A new reception counter, a simple monolithic design, directs visitors into the open gallery space from the main entry, highlighting the robust character of the existing building envelope in which it sits.

The work–life balance is an important consideration in this contemporary architectural office. Its close proximity to beaches, parks and the harbour sees its energetic staff group undertaking activities such as surfing, swimming, walking, jogging and cycling before hours, after hours and during lunch times. An area was incorporated adjacent to the park entry for the storage of 15 bicycles, surfboards and other sporting gear.

Environmentally sustainable design elements include green screen wall plantings of bamboo within workstation areas, which absorb and filter emissions from computers, photocopiers and other electrical equipment. They also act as informal privacy screens between workstations and meeting or studio spaces.

1

1 Reception gallery space: simple, monolithic, warming and inviting

2 Adaptive reuse: linked levels weave through the historic building fabric while bamboo plantings absorb and filter harmful emissions

2

3

4

3 The work–life balance: smart storage makes work, exercise and lifestyle a convenience

4 Integrated multimedia boardroom: high-tech innovation meets traditional material palette

5 Formal and informal: meeting and design studio zones integrate

6 Breakout and think: active meeting spaces without disruption

7 Staff work spaces: modern flexibility, practical functionality

Photography: Tyrone Branigan

5

6

7

The Juggernaut Offices

Toronto, Ontario, Canada

Giannone Petricone Associates

Expanding on the normally hermetic conditions of a post-production studio, the architect designed four private 'living room' studio suites, a corridor of open workstations and a reception area that offers itself as a social hub, flexibly shifting into a lunchroom, meeting room or entertainment space.

Occupying the ground floor of a historic warehouse building in downtown Toronto, the existing structure was left intact, becoming a sheath for a new lining of suspended plywood ribbons, laminated on either side with rubber and plastic. The ribbons line the interior of the existing 330-square-metre warehouse space, creating surfaces for lounging, lunching, storage and display. Layers of drywall, glass, Venetian plaster, glazed tile and walnut millwork create a rich textural palette evocative of the creative and energetic 'cutting and splicing' work for which the company is known.

The architect's additive approach provides intrigue from the exterior and dramatically transforms and enlivens the interior. The ribbons encircle the reception space like giant film strips, transitioning into built-in seating, countertops and surfaces for display, and behind the reception they splice into a pillow-like wall of Venetian plaster that 'oozes' out from the edges of the ribbons. A single ribbon 'morphs' into a counter, and returns as a small shelf in the depths of the plaster wall. The ribbons offer framed views of the raw fabric of timber and brick, and shield the deficiencies of the building while enabling light.

Inspired by the rows of computer monitors required for editing work, the architect punctured walnut cabinetry with steel-framed light boxes that display custom-designed artwork and sequences by The Juggernaut. The screens offer multiple views of the same image, and then collapse into a single frame, adding a kinetic and spectacular effect while highlighting the nature of the client's work.

1 Reception desk with waxed steel panoramic video screen
2 View of reception area with servery and bar

3

4

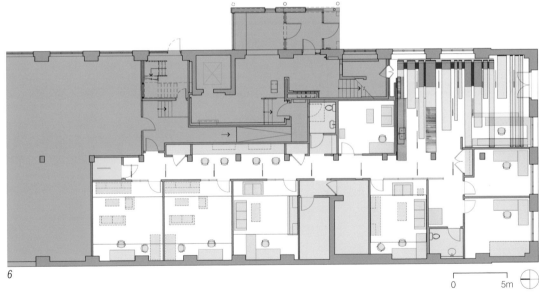

3 The ribbons as screening elements to exterior daylight

4 Ribbons folding to become bar and server elements

5 One of the four private 'living room' editing suites

6 Floor plan

0   5m

Photography: Ben Rahn, A-Frame

The White Agency

Sydney, New South Wales, Australia
Siren Design Group

This project marked an exciting time for The White Agency, with an office relocation coinciding with the launch of its new branding. The space had to make a statement to showcase the firm's strengths as an advertising agency specialising in cutting-edge digital advertising that is daring, alternative, innovative and 'outside-the-box'. With the bold contrast of black and white as the base palette, colour punctuates the space through painted vertical surface features, joinery details and furniture selection – injecting doses of The White Agency's personality throughout the space.

The design concept was based on the firm's core values of the importance of staying transparent, functional and energetic. The rope feature is a play on the 'hands on' approach, while cleverly doubling as functional space dividers. This meets the key requirement of being in an inclusive open-plan environment, without any separation between the 'creatives' and upper management. Other features include a large breakout space/function area with a range of fun activities such as foosball and Playstation, where staff can meet, greet, play and eat.

With this project Siren Design had the privilege of fitting out the first floor of this beautifully restored heritage-listed building, originally built in 1938. The open-plan design really maximises the natural ventilation and light that comes through the space, all the way from the striking curved blackbutt ceiling down to the re-buffed concrete floor.

1

1 Reception counter and waiting area viewed from entry point

2 Customised black and white rug inspired by company's new branding

2

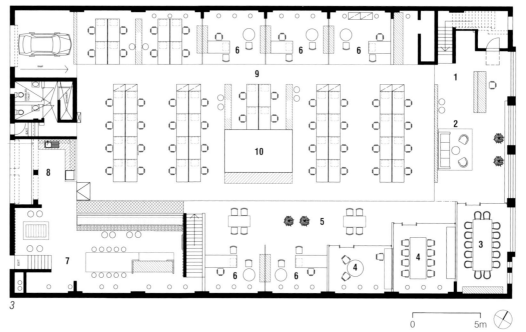

1 Reception
2 Waiting area
3 Boardroom
4 Meeting room
5 Platform area
6 Office
7 Breakout area
8 Kitchen
9 Workstation area
10 Void

0   5m

3

4

5

6

3 Floor plan

4 Creative storage and casual meeting solutions used to enhance flexibility

5 Featured rope divider allows for an open-plan environment

6 Natural light-filled open workspace

Photography: Michael Gliatis of Product Photography Studio

Volkswagen Group of America US Headquarters

Herndon, Virginia, USA

VOA Associates

This six-storey, 17,000-square-metre building in Herndon, Virginia was chosen as the location of Volkswagen's new U.S. headquarters. From the outset, the architects worked closely with Volkswagen Group of America to create a unique design representative of its new culture, to enable Volkswagen to attract top-calibre talent to its new facility while providing a showcase for the brand.

The interior of the existing building was dramatically changed, including the creation of a new central interconnecting staircase between the second and sixth floors. Designed to promote interaction between the various departments, the interconnecting stair visually and physically connects all of the floors above the ground level. The stair, which when viewed from above can be seen as a representation of Volkswagen's silver logo, also acts as a vertical exhibition space allowing for a multimedia display of brands.

Showrooms displaying the latest designs of Volkswagen's major brands were located at the front entrance to emphasise the importance of the quality of the product to its customer base. The entire facility acts as a showcase for Volkswagen by incorporating the vibrant, lively, youthful images the brand represents into the look and feel of the space. From flooring to finishes to the look of the custom workstations, the overall design is meant to be an abstract representation of the automobile body.

In moving from a more traditional private office environment to a new, more collaborative workplace culture, the client and design team emphasised open workstations with few private offices. Coffee break lounges and teaming rooms are included on every floor, with a large open staff cafeteria included on the first floor. The result is a more engaging work environment with maximum daylighting, reduced energy requirements and a highly efficient floorplan.

1

2

3

4

4 Atrium

5 Volkswagen showroom lounge

6 First floor plan

7 Cafeteria

Photography: Nick Merrick – Hedrich Blessing

5

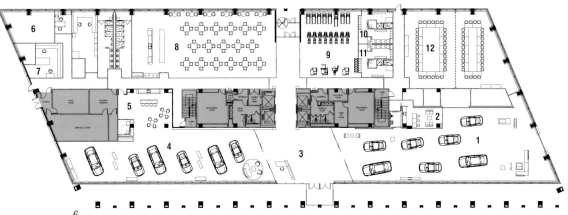

1 Audi vehicle showroom
2 Audi showroom lounge
3 Lobby
4 VW vehicle showroom
5 VW showroom lounge
6 Film studio
7 Mail room
8 Cafeteria
9 Fitness centre
10 Men's locker room
11 Women's locker room
12 Conference room

0   10m

6

7

WGV Versicherungen – Customer Service Centre

Stuttgart, Baden-Württemberg, Germany

Ippolito Fleitz Group

The WGV insurance group's new headquarters is located in Stuttgart's city centre. It incorporates a roomy 1000 square metres of open space, which is distinguished by maximum acoustic discretion.

Presenting the company to the outside world, a light wall communicates the group's corporate colour. In their highly visible corner situation, this wall and a prominent triad of conference islands convey a strong visual accent. The curved façade leads visitors around to the main entrance area, which is clearly marked by a projecting canopy.

The ground floor functions as a customer service area, where reception, work and waiting areas merge seamlessly. The terrazzo floor and ceiling-guide elements establish an additional link between these areas. Individual customer service desks are ordered sequentially within the open, elongated space. The table elements project in a continued band towards the ceiling, ensuring maximum spatial and acoustic discretion as a result of their enclosed form and materiality. The ceiling and lighting design provide the spacious room with additional visual rhythm.

1

2

3

4

1 Reception desk; the light wall in the background reflects the group's corporate colour

2 Waiting area

3 Wing with enclosed claims office

4 Three meeting pods are designed to give privacy to life-insurance clients

5 Agents sit at eight uniquely shaped custom desks

Photography: Zooey Braun

5

Wittlinger Hahn Stern Radiology

Schorndorf, Baden-Württemberg, Germany

Ippolito Fleitz Group

This radiology practice is designed to address its patients' moods and situations in a highly sensitive way. The waiting rooms convey a sense of security, the orientation system is designed to make wayfinding straightforward and the technological apparatus remains largely hidden, providing patients with a greater sense of security. The layout of the practice is organised around the patients' waiting area, which is located at the centre. The functional areas for nuclear medicine, MRI and CRi, x-ray, mammography and ultrasound are grouped around it, making a labyrinthine system of corridors obsolete. Distances between the treatment rooms and waiting area are so small that a loudspeaker system is not required, making communication direct and personal.

The two reception areas are contained in partially enclosed units to the left and right of the entrance area, allowing maximum discretion. The central waiting area is characterised by four symmetrical columns that merge with the ceiling via a concave cavetto. The side walls are upholstered from floor to ceiling and curve into the room at their upper ends, thereby positively enclosing those waiting and giving them a feeling of protection and security.

Since no natural light enters the windowless waiting area, the freestanding walls that back onto the reception area have a secondary function as a light source. They are backlit and display black-and-white images of clouds, inviting visitors to meditate on the endless expanse of sky and providing a powerful symbol of hope. Moreover, the black-and-white design brings an archetypal x-ray image to mind.

Three consulting rooms are located behind the partition for private patients. To signal the open attitude of the doctors towards the patients, each one has a glass façade onto the corridor, which can be darkened if required.

This project won the iF communication design award 2008 and is nominated for the Design Award of the Federal Republic of Germany 2010.

1

1 Reception

2 Freestanding walls backing onto the reception area function as a light source for the waiting area

3 Waiting patients can choose between a row of seating along one of the two sidewalls or a ring encircling each of the four columns

4 The waiting area is characterised by four symmetrical columns that merge with the ceiling via a concave cavetto

2

3

4

5   Floor plan

6   Wardrobe and reception station designed for
    more sensitive admissions procedures

7   The colour concept supports the different
    functions of the individual areas

8   Separate waiting area for private patients

Photography: Zooey Braun

1   Wardrobe
2   Reception
3   Waiting room
4   Waiting room for private patients
5   Surgery
6   Ultrasound
7   Mammogram
8   X-ray
9   Computed tomography
10 MRI
11 Nuclear medicine
12 Nuclear medicine waiting room

5

6

7

Yello Branding Agency

Sydney, New South Wales, Australia

Cullen Feng Pty Ltd

This project demonstrates the successful and cost-effective design of a sustainable contemporary studio for a prominent national design agency using minimal new resources. Yello's aim is to be the boldest branding agency in the country.

The two-level studio is in an inner-city post-industrial warehouse building. The original building fabric contributed well-used timber floors, exposed steel columns, trusses and a voluminous sawtooth roof.

The design is a gallery-like series of spaces within the industrial shell. The spaces are tied together by the meta-concept of the office as a continuous gallery space on which the studio themselves have or will apply graphic treatments that are part of the branding of the business – these are striking, dramatic, fun, enigmatic and often over-the-top, a work in progress.

The gallery aesthetic is most obvious in the meeting room and reception area, which have compressed fibre cement floors, evoking concrete gallery floors. A plasma screen is recessed into the wall behind a sheer curtain like a multimedia installation while a medieval aperture modulates different daylight qualities into the space. A large glass 'yelloboard' floats on one wall and provides an erasable writing board and a magnetic surface on which to pin up sketches and prints.

The upstairs reception area juxtaposes a warped antique desk with state-of-the-art computers and an oversize yellow rectangle. The office areas behind accommodate production, client service and administration functions and are flooded with natural light from above.

The design studio and an adjacent resource library are downstairs. Also on this level is a kitchen/flexible studio space that houses a compactus for sample storage (graphics on the compactus make it resemble giant books) and room for the occasional photo shoot or office party.

1

1   Waiting area with custom lounge and graphics
2   Boardroom with recessed plasma screen

2

3

4

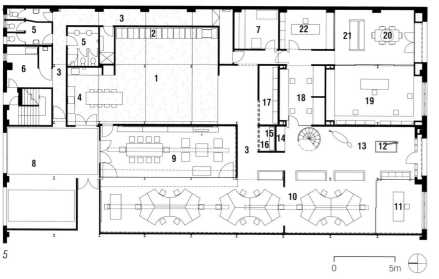

5

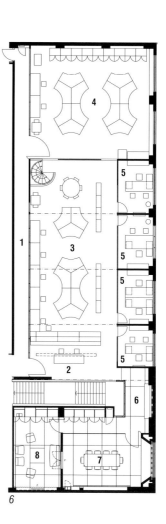

6

1 Flexible studio space
2 Compactus storage
3 Corridor
4 Café
5 Restrooms
6 Kitchen
7 Production
8 Loading dock
9 Library
10 Design studio
11 Design director
12 Billiards
13 Breakout
14 Existing display
15 Data
16 Servers
17 Store
18 Creative directors
19 Managing director
20 Meeting
21 Office assistant
22 Office

1 Intertenancy hallway
2 Reception
3 Client service
4 Operations
5 Office
6 Waiting
7 Boardroom
8 Teamroom

0   5m

7

8

3 Office area with meeting room beyond

4 Kitchen/café/studio with giant book compactus

5 Ground floor plan

6 First floor plan

7 Reception with recycled timber desk

8 Meeting room with offices beyond

Photography: Eric Sierins

Index of Architects

Index of Architects continued